PAGAN PRIDE

PAGAN PRIDE

Honoring the Craft and Culture of Earth and Goddess

M. Macha NightMare

CITADEL PRESS
Kensington Publishing Corp.
www.kensingtonbooks.com

CITADEL PRESS BOOKS are published by

Kensington Publishing Corp.
850 Third Avenue
New York, NY 10022

All Kensington titles, imprints, and distributed lines are available at special quantity discounts for bulk purchases for sales promotions, premiums, fund-raising, educational, or institutional use. Special book excerpts or customized printings can also be created to fit specific needs. For details, write or phone the office of the Kensington special sales manager: Kensington Publishing Corp., 850 Third Avenue, New York, NY 10022, attn: Special Sales Department; phone: 1-800-221-2647.

First Printing: September 2004

10 9 8 7 6 5 4 3 2 1

Printed in the United States of America

Library of Congress Control Number: 2004106005

ISBN 0-8065-2548-7

Dedicated to the Memory of

Judy Foster—Calypso Iris
November 2, 1932–October 8, 2000

Tim John Maroney
October 28, 1961–July 3, 2003

and

Harry McBride—Belenus 2*
March 7, 1941–December 27, 2003

Contents

Acknowledgments

The creation of this book surprised me at every turn. When I really stopped to think about the notion of Pagan pride—what Pagans of all kinds have contributed to world culture and society—the overall picture grew broader and deeper. The more I thought about it, and talked about it with other Pagans and Witches, whom I call my Pagan co-religionists, the longer my list of entries grew. And, like the effects of a magic spell, the book changed itself—and me—and I hope it will change you, the reader. Most of these friends wanted to see a book that they could proudly share with friends and relatives of other faiths, their Pagan co-religionists, as well as with their colleagues in local, regional, national, and international interfaith. They believed, and they convinced me, that today's Pagans, and people interested in Pagans and Paganism, would love to learn about the many incredible achievements of our Pagan ancestors. To the two friends who persuaded me that people would appreciate information about Pagan contributions to society and culture, Don Frew and Anna Korn, I offer my gratitude.

Early in the process the following people helped with overview and organization: Magenta Griffin, Leon Reed, Michael York, Jennifer LaVoie, Laura Wildman, Cat Chapin-Bishop, Lowell McFarland, and Vibra Eirene Willow.

For coming through in a pinch in their respective areas of expertise, I thank Denice Okana Szafran, spinner of both stories and webs and a practitioner of Polonia folk magic; Sean Folsom, piper's piper, with a collection of more than 250 bagpipes from all countries and ages; brewer Dave Magenet; craftswoman Willow Polson; and globe-trotter M. A. Bovis. I thank Patricia Monaghan for professional counsel and ongoing encouragement. For triple duty, I thank Celtic reconstructionist Erynn Rowan Laurie; and for performance above and beyond friendship, Victoria Slind-Flor, who has a multitude of dazzling talents, and amazing tolerance for my neurotic ramblings.

I thank Bob Shuman for his continued enthusiasm and extraordinary patience. To my ever-supportive agent, Jennie Dunham, a tip of my pointy black hat.

And last, but first in my heart, thanks to my partner Corby Lawton, for feeding and caring, patience and encouragement, and late-night, head-clearing walks in the lush, redwood-studded hills of our neighborhood.

Blessings of the living land,
M. Macha NightMare
San Rafael, California
September 2003

Introduction

P A G A N. One simple five-letter word with so many meanings!

Etymologically, *pagan* comes from the Latin *pagus*, which originally meant "something stuck in the ground as a landmark." The Latin *paganus* means a villager or rustic. Pagan came to mean a country dweller, an unsophisticated rural person who relied more directly on the land, Nature, and her gifts of food, clothing, and shelter. In short, a hick. Related words are the English *peasant*, one who lives and works on the land; the French *le pays*, or countryside, among many others. Calling someone a pagan in the ancient world meant that this person, a villager or a rustic, had none of the refinements of civilization. It also came to mean a civilian other than Roman militia. Unlike armies of Roman soldiers, Pagans lived and worked on the land, and didn't travel.

Another word that is often used either with the word pagan or as a synonym for pagan is *heathen*. Similar to a pagan, who lives in the *pagus* (rural district), a heathen is a person who dwells on the heath. A heath is an open, uncultivated tract of land with sandy soil covered with rough grasses and shrubs. To call someone a heathen was meant to be insulting, and meant that the person did "not acknowledge the God of the Bible, Torah, or Koran." Heathen could refer to a person who had no religion, hence, like a pagan, was considered to be uncivilized.

Reclamation of the Words Pagan and Heathen Today

"Neopaganism is a highly varied mixture of ancient and modern elements, in which nature worship (influenced by modern environmentalism) often plays a major role. Other influences include shamanism, magical and occult traditions, and radical feminist critiques of Christianity" (*The New Oxford American Dictionary,* Oxford University Press, 2001).

I tend to use the word *Pagan* to describe those people, like myself, considered to be "NeoPagan." I do this because NeoPagan implies that there were more or less unified movements of "PaleoPaganism" (an ancient, more or less unified Pagan religion) and "MesoPaganism" (a more current, more recent, perhaps more sophisticated unified Pagan religion). We have no evidence that such was the case.

Today, the word Pagan is generally used to mean religions that are not Abrahamic (descending from the patriarch Abraham). Paganism represents a different "way" of being religious from that of the revealed religions, those "based on divine revelation rather than reason." Revealed religions have books and commandments and other rules and laws that come from some other "outside" authority, such as Yahweh. This use of the word Pagan includes NeoPagans, but it also includes indigenous and tribal religions and Earth- and Nature-based spiritualities as well as ancestor-reverence and shamanism. Along with the NeoPagans such as Witches and Druids, the broader use of the term Pagan can be said to

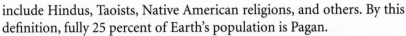

include Hindus, Taoists, Native American religions, and others. By this definition, fully 25 percent of Earth's population is Pagan.

Further, many, if not most, [Neo]Pagans are captivated by history, anthropology, mythology, science fiction, and other areas of study. A look at the books on the shelves in Pagan households, an analysis of our book-buying and reading habits, and our levels of formal education lend credence to the statement that Paganism is perhaps one of the most educated religions on the planet. In the increasingly multicultural United States, Pagans successfully organize with one another, in many cases using consensus process drawn from the practices of the Society of Friends (Quakers). Top-down, highly stratified hierarchies are less and less common within Pagan culture, and usually only operate in small working groups such as covens, circles, or traditions. The larger organizations having to do with Pagan civil rights, such as the Covenant of the Goddess (CoG), Alternative Religions Education Network (AREN), Pagan Educational Network (PEN) , and Our Freedom: A Pagan Civil Rights Coalition are very egalitarian in both organization and process.

Since the convening of the Council for the Parliament of World Religions in Chicago in 1993, with the goal of "cultivat[ing] harmony between the world's religious and spiritual communities and foster[ing] their engagement with the world and its other guiding institutions in order to achieve a peaceful, just, and sustainable world," Pagans of all kinds, including NeoPagans, have been a recognized part of the American religious scene. Pagans moved from "fringe group" to "religious minority."

Pagans are an active presence in the Parliament and in another international interfaith organization, the United Religions Initiative, and in the North American Interfaith Network as well as in regional and local interfaith bodies.

All Witches Are Pagans but Not All Pagans Are Witches

The most popular of the many NeoPagan religious paths is Witchcraft. There are more Witches and Wiccans than there are practitioners of other Pagan paths such as Druidry or Asatru. Sometimes the noun "Wicca" is used as a synonym for Witchcraft but they are not exactly the same. The practices of Wiccans are taught and inherited in a lineage or lineages that come from Britain. They are sometimes referred to as British traditional Witches. The most well known among the British traditions is Gardnerian Witchcraft, which traces to a British civil servant named Gerald Gardner and his coveners and associates. Another British tradition is Alexandrian, coming from a man named Alex Sanders and made popular by one of his initiates, the late Stewart Farrar. British traditions work in small covens with a high priestess and high priest, and they acknowledge levels of training, skill development, and understanding for which they "elevate" the person to a higher degree. Other American Wiccan traditions are those inspired by the writings of Englishman Robert Cochran, also known as Roy Bowers; they are the Clan of Tubal Cain and 1734 tradition.

Besides the British traditions, there are bootstrap traditions, Dianic

Witches who worship goddesses only, reconstructionist traditions based on Norse, Greek, or Celtic deities, symbolisms, and concepts. Witches working within an Italian framework call themselves *strega* or *stregaria*, the Italian word for Witch. Contemporary Brazilian Witches are *bruxos* (male) and *bruxas* (female). The adjective that I use for things related to Witchcraft and Wicca is "Witchen."

If that isn't complicated enough, there are many individuals and groups who have blended their Witchen and/or Pagan practices with other faith traditions. Among them are Buddheo-Pagans, Jewitches, Quagans (Quaker Pagans), and Christo-Pagans. The Internet has facilitated the development of cyberritual (ritual done online, in cyberspace) and cybermagic (magic spells done online, in cyberspace), hence cyber-Pagans, techno-Pagans.

Druidry is primarily a reconstructed ethnic religion derived from the ancient Celtic tribal religion. Asatru comes from Northern Europe and is considered, by its adherents, to be more of an ethnic religion than a Nature religion, as most Pagan paths are. Romuva, the ancient Pagan religion of the Baltic regions, is widespread in that area and has practitioners in the United States as well. Polonia is Polish folk religion, also Pagan. Practioners or reconstructionists of ancient Egyptian religion are called Kemetics.

Some contemporary Pagan religions are proudly and lovingly reconstructed. Followers of reconstructionist paths do academic research; draw on family customs, anthropology, folklore and traditions, archaeology, and history; and learn from their own experiences and intuition to create practices and belief systems that have deep meaning for them. These practices reinforce a sense of connectedness to our ancestors and help make sense of the world, just as any religion does. In addition to Druidry and Asatru, the most commonly found reconstructionist religion is Hellenic, the traditions of Iron Age through Classical Greece.

I am using the word "Pagan" in the context of this book to mean all Pagan religions, but more particularly those Pagan religions originating in the Mediterranean, North Africa, the Middle East, that passed—with human commerce and migration—through Eastern, Central, and Western Europe, and on to the United States. These religions, or revivals of them, or religions drawing on these ancient Pagan cults, are alive today in the English-speaking countries of Canada, Australia, and New Zealand, as well as throughout Europe. There are places in Europe where they have never died. They are also in Iceland, Brazil, and Japan.

I hope you will be surprised, and encouraged, by how much Pagans and Paganism have contributed to society and culture. Every day, what we take for granted, such as agriculture, art, architecture, medicine, brewing, mathematics, and textiles, all have their source in Paganism.

PAGAN PRIDE

I

ART AND LITERATURE, FOLKLORE AND FOLKWAYS

Ancient Pagan art forms can be seen around us today, produced in glass, fabric sculpture, metalwork, plastic, tattoos, and artifacts of all kinds. We see a bracelet of Egyptian scarabs on a Kemetic friend, Celtic and Saxon interlace designs adorning those of all religions.

We speak of Trojan horses; we even have "Trojan horses" in cyberculture, not to mention a well-known brand of Trojan condoms. We shave our legs with Venus razors, supposed to enhance our sex appeal. Our physician's door is marked with a caduceus, the wand of Mercury.

Seldom do we realize how many stories and tales that we

know so well are the same ones that have been told by human beings around hearth fires for thousands of years. Whether they
come to us clothed in their original garments or have been put into
contemporary settings, these stories are told over and over to successive generations. Further, they may change with ethnic migration and contact with the stories of other human groups. Yet they
endure as mythology and folklore. Many also form the founda-
tions of our diverse contemporary Pagan practices.

1

The *Aenead*

The wanderings and adventures of Aeneas are chronicled in an epic written by the Roman poet Virgil in the first century B.C.E. Virgil consciously imitated the earlier Greek poet Homer in constructing twelve volumes of tales of the hero, Aeneas, in his wanderings after the Trojan War chronicled by him. Aeneas is a Trojan and the stalwart companion of the doomed Trojan warrior Hector. Being a son of the goddess Aphrodite, Aeneas is much favored by the Olympians. Thus when he is wounded and in danger on the battlefield, the god Apollo causes a cloud to envelop him, and the goddess Artemis heals him.

After Troy's defeat by the Greeks, the brave, resourceful hero flees the city, taking along his family and some friends, carrying his aged father, Anchises, on his back. Aeneas also takes with him all the family's Lares—statues of the Roman household deities who protect the house and family within. Every Roman household had at least one small statue of its Lares. These statues were placed in high places or on the roof. A statue also sat on the dining table, taking part in the domestic happenings by its presence. Aeneas also takes all the Penates, meaning carvings "with a penis." These were similar to Lares in being household gods, except that they guarded the storeroom. Statues of Penates always have overlarge penises and stood above the entrance or on the roof of villas.

Aeneas wanders the Mediterranean region and loses his wife as well as his father over the course of his journey. A storm drives his ship to the coast of Africa, where the queen of Carthage, Dido, falls in love with him. He tarries with Dido, until Hermes brings an order from the gods that Aeneas must leave Carthage and continue his journey to fulfill his destiny. The abandoned queen kills herself. Later, Aeneas travels to the Underworld of Hades through an opening at Cumae (near present-day Naples), where he speaks with his dead father and realizes that his destiny lies in Rome. While there, Aeneas also speaks with the shade (ghost) of Dido, but she cannot forgive him.

Aeneas eventually reaches Latium (from which our adjective "Latin"). The king, Latinus, welcomes the Trojan refugees and offers Aeneas his daughter, Lavinia, in marriage. Aeneas thus becomes the ancestor of the Roman people: Romulus and Remus, the feral twins suckled by a wolf, descend from Aeneas through their mother, the priestess Rhea Silvia. Julius Caesar's family, Gens Julia, trace their lineage to one of Aeneas's sons. When Aeneas died, he was defied and worshipped under the name of Indiges (from the Latin word meaning "to beget," from which we get our word "indigenous"), suggesting that his worshippers considered him to be their progenitor.

We can see from Virgil's recountings that he intended his Aeneas to model a pious, righteous man, one who is devoted to his parents and family, to the gods, and to the destiny of Rome, the city with which he is ultimately associated. Aeneas exemplified the Roman quality of *pietas*, the concept that gives us our words "piety" and "pious."

See **The *Iliad*, Aphrodite, Cumaean Sybil.**

2

Baba Yaga

The old Witch Baba Yaga lives deep in the swampy birch forests of old Russia. Her hut is mounted on chicken legs. Inside, she sleeps on a brick oven—the same oven she uses to cook—and when she lies down to sleep, her nose reaches the ceiling. Her hut is surrounded by a fence made of the bones of those whose flesh she's devoured with her iron teeth. Many skulls with blazing eye sockets stare out from the top of the fence posts. Imagine what a frightening site this is to anyone who comes upon it in the darkness of the woods. Baba Yaga needs only to look out the window to scare her victims to death.

Her hut doesn't remain in one place, but instead moves about the forest on its scrawny chicken legs. It can move in all directions—backward and forward, up and down, and in circles—all with hideous, hair-raising sounds of creaking and screeching. When it is still, the hut faces away from visitors unless they know a secret incantation. If they do, then it spins around and comes to a stop in front of the visitor, then opens its door.

Though her hut is small, it accommodates Baba Yaga's faithful servants. Her work is done by three bodiless pairs of hands she calls "my soul friends." Her other magical servants are the White Horseman, the Red Horseman, and the Black Horseman. They are her Bright Dawn, her Red Sun, and her Dark Midnight.

Baba Yaga isn't always at home, though, and to get around she has a unique vehicle. She flies through the sky in a mortar, propelling herself with a pestle and then sweeping away her trail with a broom.

The blue-nosed Baba Yaga orders the cycles of Nature. By turns, she is frenzied and violent like a storm, and kind and helpful as a sunny day. This paradoxical hag is the ancient Slavic goddess of death and rebirth. She offers advice, help, and wisdom to those who approach her with respect and without fear despite her terrifying aspect. To the pure of heart she gives advice and magical gifts. When we suffer depression and ennui, we enter the neighborhood of Baba Yaga's magical hut, the place where we may be transformed if we meet her. Her skulls burn with inner flame to enlighten the path through the forest of life.

Baba Yaga is a powerful figure for women of all ages, especially for those beyond the age of reproduction.

3

Bagpipes

The history of bagpipes, that strangest of musical instruments—made from the bladders of animals and reeds from the marshes—is shrouded in mystery. After all bagpipes are an instrument made and played by peasants (hicks, country dwellers, pagans), who lived much of their lives out of doors in rustic circumstances and weren't typically well educated. Shepherds and farmers, people directly connected to the land, played little or no role in politics, philosophy, courtly concerns, warfare, or formal religion. These bagpipe players were of low social status, and as artisans were less likely to illustrate their lives in stone, pottery, and other media, although there are actually a few Greek depictions of pipers. But the other reason why information about bagpipes is scarce is because bagpipes were made of organic material, which tends to deteriorate over time, so there are no extant examples of the ancient instruments.

Derived from prehistoric reeded woodwind instruments, bagpipes were first played in the ancient Middle East. The grain god played the "silver pipes of Ur," called *ghie-git*. Egyptians in 1800 B.C.E. played a bagpipe called the *ma-it*. The infamous Emperor Nero threatened to play the bagpipe if he lost a certain wager, and Roman legions are believed to have marched to their shrill wail. It may have been the Romans who spread the bagpipe throughout Europe.

There is great diversity of the bagpipe and its predecessors. The bagpipe played for dances and public events allowed one single piper who could fill the air with loud, rich music. Each country had is own variety of the instrument for playing its own style of folk music: Bretons dance the *bombarde*, to the music of a mouth-blown bagpipe called the *Biniou*. The bagpipe of Sweden is the *Säckpipa*, and that of Italy is the *Zampogna*. The Galicians play a bagpipe with the Spanish name *Gaita*. The Turks call their bagpipe the *Tulum*, and the Croatian *Surle* and *Diple* have two chanters (pipes with fingerholes for playing different notes) and no drone to provide a continuous background sound. All have variation in the sounds they produce, like the variations among NeoPagans throughout the world.

Scottish Great Highland bagpipes are the most familiar today, followed by the *Uillean* bagpipe of Ireland, which has three drones and is bellows-driven, allowing the player to sing. The Northumbrian Smallpipe has four drones and its design allows the player to play staccato.

The bagpipe, invention of our earth-loving Pagan ancestors, produces such a unique sound that the English have given it its very own verb: *skirl*.

4

Bards and Storytelling

Bards of many traditions and cultures are responsible for the oral preservation and transmission of language, history, genealogies, and spiritual wisdom. Encapsulated in the myths and legends, they tell of the accumulated knowledge of their people. As ethnographer Albert Bates Lord has said, "People did not wait until there was writing before they told stories and sang songs," meaning that stories existed and were passed geographically and generationally long before anyone thought to commit them to paper. From fairy tales and historical epics to songs of praise and tales of everyday life, oral traditions have been, and continue to be, an integral part of cultures everywhere.

Probably the most familiar Bardic tradition to Western civilization was that of the Celts. In the earliest Celtic tribes, the Bards were chosen from among the ruling aristocracy. They were part of the learned class of priests, teachers, and judges who were known as Druids, and their training as Master Bards was long and arduous. Roman historians write of Bardic schools where the "singers and poets" undertook up to twenty years of training.

There are Bardic traditions of other European cultures, the vestiges of which still survive. Lord studied the South Slavic epic singers whose performances resemble Homeric-sung epic. These Serbo-Croatian artists were trained by rote to repeat the thousands of lines of epic poetry that contained ancient wisdoms of their ancestors. Lithuania and Latvia have the *daina*, epic poetry that is sung or recited, which describes the sacredness of the ancient gods and the ways in which to live everyday life. An estimated twenty-nine thousand *dainos* survive today in the Latvian language.

Russian *byliny*, meaning "that which has been," weave the legends about the *bogatyri*, or "elder valiant champions." These oral ballad cycles celebrate quasi-historical figures and were told only orally until the early seventeenth century; Russian lacquer boxes almost exclusively feature scenes from these tales. Nature is personified in these oral stories: rivers, animals, and the sky itself all come to life, fragments surviving from an earlier Pagan tradition. Ritual, wedding, and harvest songs are very hard to date, but they contain invocations to the sun and the moon, and tales of the water and the winds, as well as outline seasonal celebrations and the spirits whose patronage is honored. Vestiges of these can be found still in Christianity, a perfect example of which is the "Ukrainian Carol of the Birds."

The Nibelungen Saga of Germanic peoples tells, in a 2,439-verse epic, of the rise and fall of the fourth-century Burgundian empire through the adventures of the mythical hero Siegfried/Sigurd. Austrian researchers uncovered a written version of the epic that dates to the twelfth century, yet the written version is substantially different from the epic told from generation to generation. From Finland comes the Kalevala, their national epic. There are epic tales preserved orally in China, African nations, and among Australian and North American indigenous peoples.

"The marvel of oral tradition, some will say its curse, is this: messages from the past exist, are real, and yet are not continuously accessible to the senses. Oral traditions make an appearance only when they are told. For fleeting moments they can be heard, but most of the time they dwell only in the minds of people. The utterance is transitory, but the memories are not. No one in oral societies doubts that memories can be faithful repositories that contain the sum total of past human experience and explain the how and why of present-day conditions. Whether memory changes or not, culture is reproduced by remembrance put into words and deeds. The mind through memory carries culture from generation to generation" (Jan Vansina).

See **The *Poetic Eddas* and the *Nibelungenlied,* The *Kalevala.***

5

Beowulf

Beowulf is the earliest epic poem written in English, albeit one difficult for most contemporary English speakers to understand. Although the poem was written on a manuscript around 1000 C.E., the events it describes took place about five hundred years earlier. Like many epics, the story of Beowulf is probably an accumulation and weaving together of several tales.

Beowulf, whose name means "bear wolf," was a member of the seafaring tribe called the Geats from the south of Sweden. He was born around the year 495 C.E. The epic opens with Beowulf and a small band of his companions crossing the sea to Denmark to help his kinsman, Hrothgar, rid his country of a monster that has been terrorizing his people.

Gigantic Grendel, the strong, smelly, ugly monster has been coming to the hall and killing and eating Hrothgar's warriors for many years. He refuses to accept the tributes of gold Hrothgar offers; he refuses to negotiate peace. Grendel disdains all law and custom. Not only is he strong, but his body is impervious to normal wounds. Now, in the dark,

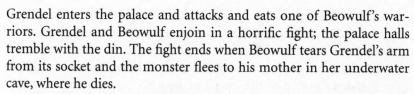

Grendel enters the palace and attacks and eats one of Beowulf's warriors. Grendel and Beowulf enjoin in a horrific fight; the palace halls tremble with the din. The fight ends when Beowulf tears Grendel's arm from its socket and the monster flees to his mother in her underwater cave, where he dies.

The following night, Grendel's vile mother, more foul and hideous than her son, seeks to avenge her son. She attacks Hrothgar's palace, kills the king's advisor, and escapes. Beowulf pursues her to her den, called Unferth, where, with a magic sword named Naegling forged by the giants themselves, Beowulf does battle with the water troll. He beheads both her and the dead Grendel lying in a corner, but their blood is so hot it melts even that blade, leaving only the hilt in Beowulf's hand.

Beowulf delivers the heads to Hrothgar. The Danes shower praise and gifts upon Beowulf and his warriors, and they return to their homeland. There, upon the death of his uncle Heardred in 533 C.E., Beowulf is crowned king. Much loved by his subjects, he rules in peace for half a century. Then as an old man who has proven himself an able leader, distributing weapons and treasure wisely, the peace is disturbed again by an enraged, fire-breathing dragon.

This time, accompanied by his brave young kinsman Wiglaf, Beowulf manages to overcome the beast with his bare hands, although his sword breaks on the dragon's scaly body. Wiglaf delivers the fatal blow as Beowulf lies dying. Beowulf gives Wiglaf his ring, his boar-headed helmet, and his suit of armor, then dies. Thus ends Beowulf's heroic career.

The 1939 excavation of a seventh-century buried ship at Sutton Hoo in Suffolk, England, gives evidence of the values and customs of the people of Beowulf's time. The intricately decorated swords and other elaborate grave goods found in the ship are uncannily like those in the descriptions of the burial of Beowulf and his contemporaries. Although the noble Geats seem to have disappeared, the tales of their great king Beowulf live to this day.

6

Caduceus

Everyone recognizes the Pagan symbol of the winged wand wound with two snakes that adorns hospitals and doctors' offices. The original Greek word for the caduceus is *Kerykeion*, which means the magic rod of Hermes, messenger of the gods.

Just how the caduceus came to be associated with the healing arts is unknown, but there are several theories. One is that it represents the magician Hermes—messenger, trickster, and thief—who wore a winged helmet and winged sandals, and carried a rod topped by a knob and wound with two snakes twining upwards and crossing six times, culminating in wings. Another Greek figure, Aesculapius, a son of the god Apollo, was trained by the centaur Chiron to be a healer. So great were his healing powers that over time he acquired a cult and his temples were considered divine. Aesculapius is pictured carrying a long staff of cypress, representing strength, twined by a single snake. The god's temples, where people went for healing, contained Aesculapeian snakes in his honor; later this practice spread along with the Roman Empire from Southern Europe to the Roman temples in Germany and Austria. The connection between Hermes and Aesculapius is that Hermes delivered the infant Aesculapius from his murdered mother, Coronis.

Because snakes periodically shed their skin and seem to be reborn makes them an apt symbol for healing and regeneration. To the ancient Babylonians, twined snakes represented fertility, wisdom, and healing. Sumerian and Babylonian art is filled with half-human, half-snake figures and winged discs representing the gods.

In yoga, the primal energy of the body, called *Kundalini*—meaning "the serpent power"—is said to reside at the base of the spine. Kundalini can be stimulated or awakened by various yogic practices, and when it is released, it travels up the spine through the chakras (wheels, energy vortices) by way of two twined snakes, the *Ida* and the *Pingala*. When it has arisen through each of the six chakras, the kundalini energy awakens higher consciousness, or cosmic awareness. This experience produces a mystical sense of oneness, often described as white light or clear light.

The snakes of the caduceus, which cross six times and culminate in wings, can be seen to parallel this ancient Hindu concept.

The juxtaposition of serpents and birds is actually widespread throughout many times and places. Teutonic myth contains Yggdrassil—the World Tree—an ash with its base surrounded by the serpent Nidhogg and an eagle atop its branches. Movements in the Chinese martial art of Kung Fu are based on the motions of a crane fighting a snake, merging serpent and bird. One of the most significant gods of Mexico is Quetzalcoatl, depicted as a feathered serpent. Dragons, or winged serpents, appear throughout European and Asian legend.

The imagery in the caduceus can also be seen as symbolizing the connectedness of the worlds below and above—the snake being the underworld, the watery unconscious; the tree rooted below and reaching high, the middle world, life here and now; and the wings the upper world of spirit and cosmic consciousness. When these cosmic connections are strong, they are in their optimal state. Thus, the snakes climbing the staff and rising to wings can be a symbol of optimal health, or healing.

Greek ambassadors and heralds carried the caduceus to other lands believing it would ensure their safety. In Rome it symbolized truce and neutrality. In the sixteenth century the caduceus was a symbol of medicine throughout the Western world; in 1902, the medical branch of the U.S. Army adopted it as their symbol; and today the caduceus is recognized universally for all who practice healing arts.

See **Mercury/Hermes, Asclepius, Yggdrassil.**

7

Corn Dollies

The making of corn dollies is another surviving pagan folk art. When Americans speak of corn, they mean maize, but in the English language corn simply means any kind of grain. Thus when we speak of corn dollies, we mean many kinds of objects and designs woven of wheat or other grasses.

Of the four main sources of straw—wheat, rye, oats, and barley—wheat provides the best for making corn dollies. Wheat for making corn dollies is carefully harvested by hand with a scythe. The wheat is woven and twisted together in the forms of spirals, crosses, fans, horseshoes, stars, and it is often interwoven or decorated with ribbons, flowers, prayer rags and other materials.

The original dolly, made from the last sheaf of wheat in the field, was a straw cage in a female shape designed to capture the corn spirit. This dolly is called the harvest maiden in some regions and in others, the hag. The spirit of the corn remains in the dolly for the coming planting season.

Corn dollies are most prevalent in areas of Britain, Wales, Scotland, and Ireland, where they have also grown in complexity and sophistication, but they are made in America, too. In parts of England, the skill of making corn dollies is passed from father to son. In Scotland two dollies are made: the maiden, or *maighdean bhuana*, representing summer; and the hag, or *cailleagh*, representing winter. In Ireland, corn dollies are made of rushes and formed in the shape of crosses at the Festival of Bridget in early February to honor the goddess. "Female" corn dollies are often dressed. My own tradition uses a "Bridey dolly," dressed in white lace and bedecked with flowers, who leads the spiral dance in our annual sabbat ritual in honor of the goddess Bridget.

A popular form for corn dollies is the "harvest knot." The harvest knot for men has no seeds while a woman's harvest knot has the seeds intact, an obvious connection to fertility. Corn dollies are given as love tokens between lovers, at weddings, for house blessings, and for people moving to a new house. A dolly woven to rattle is given at the birth of or naming ceremony for a child.

Although customs and beliefs vary slightly from one region of the British Isles to another, and the dollies are called by various names (kirn or kern baby, the nec or neck, the gander's neck, the mare), they are hung in homes and barns for the rest of the year for the purpose of ensuring prosperity, good luck, and abundant harvest after the next year's growing season.

Wheat and other grain weavings are found in cultures worldwide, from Russia to Egypt, Morocco to Mexico, Asia to South America. Wherever grains began to be cultivated, humans wove them into sculptures. Probably the earliest examples are from the Fertile Crescent of the Tigris and Euphrates rivers, but since corn dollies are made from a perishable material, none survive. The Pagan tradition of crafting corn dollies survives to this day, reminding us of our dependence on the fruitfulness of Mother Earth and of the death and rebirth that comes with each turning of the Wheel.

See **Bridget, The Wheel.**

8

Cornucopia

Cornucopia means "horn of plenty." Cornu is horn, specifically a goat's horn, and Copia is one of several Roman goddesses of plenty. Actually these goddesses aren't the only ones with whom the cornucopia is associated. Depictions of Lady Fortuna, for instance, sometimes called Lady Luck and called upon by gamblers and other risk takers, is also often shown holding a cornucopia. Justitia, the Roman goddess of justice; Pax, goddess of peace; Spes, the Roman goddess of hope; Habondia,

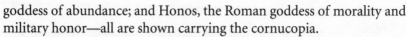

goddess of abundance; and Honos, the Roman goddess of morality and military honor—all are shown carrying the cornucopia.

The cornucopia was originally said to be a gift from the patriarch of the Greek pantheon, Zeus, to the nymph Amalthea. There are slight differences in Amalthea's story, however. In one she is a nymph who owns a goat, in another she is a nymph in the form of a goat, and in a third she is a goat. In all three versions, she was Zeus's childhood playmate. Either Amalthea or her goat had suckled the baby Zeus in a Cretan cave, and protected him from harm. One day while Zeus and Amalthea were playing, he got too exuberant and accidentally broke off one of her horns. In restitution, Zeus magically endowed the broken horn with the ability to be filled with fruits and other bounty—whatever Amalthea desired. The cornucopia symbolizes the profusion of gifts from the divine.

An alternate myth about the cornucopia tells of a fight between the strongman Hercules and the river god Achelous, son of Ocean. The god took the form of a bull when he was fighting Hercules who broke off one of the bull's horns. In appreciation for the fact that Hercules returned it, Achelous transformed the bull's horn into a horn of plenty.

We see the cornucopia today in connection with the harvest, restaurants, and merchandising. To Masons, it represents peace, plenty, and joy, all consonant with the many goddesses with whom the horn has been associated. In the United States, the Pagan cornucopia is often used as a symbol of thanksgiving, along with the turkey and people in black-and-white Puritan garb.

9

The Descent of Inanna

Inanna, Queen of Heaven, is the title by which she is best known. The Lady of Myriad Offices, or Queen of All the *Me* are others. By whatever name she is entreated, Inanna is the most important goddess in the Sumerian pantheon. Enki, god of wisdom and the waters, bestowed upon her the ten thousand *mes*, or gifts of civilization, the arts, and culture. Inanna, the Exalted Cow of Heaven, is associated with the planet Venus, the morning and the evening star.

Inanna's story is universal. It brings to mind the abduction of Demeter by Hades, the murder of Osiris by his brother Set and Isis's grief for him, and the dying and resurrected Jesus of the Christians. These stories of death and rebirth explain the cycles of the seasons and the character of the afterlife.

Inanna descends into the Underworld to answer the moaning of her sister, Ereshkigal, the realm's ruler. Inanna wears her finest clothing, with all her regalia of power, and approaches the gate of the Land of Dust. Before she enters, however, Inanna tells her handmaiden Ninshibur that if she doesn't return after three days, Ninshibur is to set up a lament for her by the ruins. "Beat the drum for me in the assembly places. Circle the houses of the Gods. Tear at your eyes, at your mouth . . . Go to Eridu, to the temple of Enki. Weep before Father Enki . . . Surely he will not let me die."

The gatekeeper to the Underworld lets her in, but at each level, or gate, Inanna is required to divest herself of one of her adornments. At the first gate, her *shugurra* or crown, symbolic of her intellect, is removed. At successive levels she leaves her earrings and the lapis beads around her neck, the bangles from her wrists and ankles, her royal breastplate covered with sparkling stones, "the girdle of birthstones around her waist, her lapis measuring rod and line," and finally, at the seventh, her robe.

Naked and alone, completely vulnerable, Inanna approaches Ereshkigal. At the urging of the Annuna, the judges of the Underworld, "her sister fastens the eye of death on Inanna." For three days and nights the dead body of the Queen of Heaven hangs alone in the dark on a meat hook, rotting, while faithful Ninshibur awaits her at the Underworld's entrance. During that time, "no bull mounted a cow, no donkey impregnated a donkey, no young man impregnated a girl." The Earth is rendered sterile.

So Ninshibur does as Inanna bade her: she seeks help from Enki. As god of action, Enki scrapes the dirt from under his fingernails and from it makes two genderless beings, the *kurgarra* and the *galatur*. He sends these beings to the Underworld with food and the water of life to revive Inanna and bring her back. Slipping through the gates, the two travel all

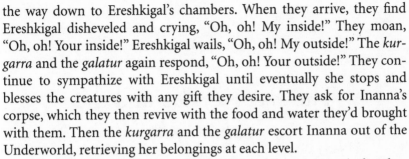

the way down to Ereshkigal's chambers. When they arrive, they find Ereshkigal disheveled and crying, "Oh, oh! My inside!" They moan, "Oh, oh! Your inside!" Ereshkigal wails, "Oh, oh! My outside!" The *kurgarra* and the *galatur* again respond, "Oh, oh! Your outside!" They continue to sympathize with Ereshkigal until eventually she stops and blesses the creatures with any gift they desire. They ask for Inanna's corpse, which they then revive with the food and water they'd brought with them. Then the *kurgarra* and the *galatur* escort Inanna out of the Underworld, retrieving her belongings at each level.

Part of the bargain between Ereshkigal and the creatures is that they find a replacement for Inanna to live in the Underworld with her. Inanna chooses Dumuzi, the lover of her youth. Dumuzi is washed with pure water, anointed with sweet oil, and clothed in a red robe in preparation for his departure. The pipers play and "the party-girls raise a loud lament." Dumuzi, god of barley and beer, will remain in the Underworld for six months of every year. When he returns each autumn, the people of the land celebrate the holy marriage feast of Inanna and Dumuzi again, the rains come and break the summer drought, renewing the fields for another year.

Many contemporary Pagans recognize Salome's dance of the seven veils as a ritual reenactment of Inanna's descent into the Underworld. We design and perform rituals based on Inanna's descent and on other stories about her.

See **Demeter and Persephone/Kore, Isis and Osiris.**

10

The *Poetic Eddas* and the *Nibelungenlied*

The *Poetic Eddas* and the *Nibelungenlied* are the two great source documents for the northern Pagan traditions. Both recount stories of the gods and the goddesses, and the interactions of heroic figures within the ancient northern world. They are as important to Nordic mythology as the Homeric poems are to our understanding of the gods and goddesses of ancient Greece, or the *Vedas* are for India's myths and legends.

The *Nibelungenlied*—which is the principal source of Wagner's Ring-series operas—is probably initially the product of singing poets from several parts of what is today Germany. They recounted the stories of the epic battles in the Age of Migration between the Burgundians—who once occupied much of what is now Germany's Rhenish Palatinate area, and the Huns. The stories got to Norway somewhere between the seventh and ninth centuries of the Common Era, probably traveling with traders or warriors. Then, when the Vikings traveled to Iceland,

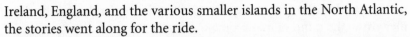

Ireland, England, and the various smaller islands in the North Atlantic, the stories went along for the ride.

They were retold in the *Eddas*, written in West Norse, which is the distinctive language that existed in the Viking world from about 800 to 1050 C.E. Many of the heroic tales showed the ancient gods in decline, probably a result of the pro-Christian bias of the writers. Still, these literary works remain important sources of information about the Nordic pantheon of both the Aesir (primarily connected with power and wars) and Vanir (mainly connected with fertility and generally peaceful) deities, including Odin, Thor, Frigg, Freya, Balder, Loki, Freyr, Idunna, Siff, and Tyr. The meaning of the word "edda" is still in dispute. Some scholars say it means "grandmother" and refers to the ancient origins of the stories. Others say the word means "poetics," and refers to the *Prose Edda* as almost a textbook on literary devices of the Viking era.

The *Eddas* contain thousands of kennings, which are poetic synonyms such as "feeder of ravens" for swords, "steeds of the sea" for ships, and "necklace glad" for Freya, the goddess associated with the glorious golden necklace Brisingamen. The first of the great *Eddas,* the "Voluspa," lays out the cosmology of the Viking world, and introduces Odin as All-Father. Odin summons the seeress—the Voluspa—from her grave—and she gives an account of the creation of the world and the first human beings, and the central position of the mighty ash tree, Yggdrasil. Another well-known poem in the *Eddas* is the "Havamal," which is, in a way, the Viking equivalent of the Emily Post guide to etiquette. Vikings loved

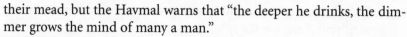

their mead, but the Havmal warns that "the deeper he drinks, the dimmer grows the mind of many a man."

The "Voluspa hin skamma" is an important eddic poem for today's Heathens—Pagans who embrace the northern traditions—because it contains phrases that are now used in oracular seidh. *Seidh* is an oracular practice using a seeress that has been revived in the last decade by Heathens in Europe and North America. The seeress (or occasionally a seer) at a Seidh session uses the words found in the Voluspa hin skamma to determine whether her listeners have heard enough, "I tell thee much, yet more lore have I. Thou needs must know this—wilt know still more?" Seidh sessions take place among many Pagans and Heathens in Western Europe and the United States.

See **The Fates, the Furies, and the Norns, Oracles and Seers, Yggdrassil.**

11

Egyptian Scarabs

Representations of scarabs (*Scarabaeus sacer*) are found throughout Egyptian art and hieroglyphic writings. They were probably sacred in the prehistoric period, given that they were found stored in jars buried with the deceased. An alabaster box shaped in the form of a scarab found in a grave confirms that scarabs were venerated at least as far back as Dynasty I. They were known in the Old Kingdom (2650–2134 B.C.E).

Ancient Egyptian texts indicate the belief that the scarab beetle came into being spontaneously from balls of dung, a characteristic they associated with their religious ideology of self-creation, resurrection, and everlasting life. They likened this to Ra rolling the ball of the sun from east to west across the sky each day and "burying" it in the darkness of night. Scarabs are dung beetles that feed on the dung of herbivores by excavating tunnels under dung heaps. With their rake-like head and front legs, they scrape and shape the dung into a ball to be heated by the sun. They roll their dung balls along with their hind legs to a suitable burial site. The female scarab embeds her eggs in the ball before burying it in the sand, where the developing larvae also feed on the dung. In appearance the scarab's wings are a beautiful iridescent blue-green. Their bodies are stout and strong, with broad, powerful, spiny legs enabling them to burrow in the soil. Although their crawl is rather inelegant, most species are strong and active flyers. The scarabs' scavenging activity has obvious benefits in terms of keeping their ecosystems viable. The beetles perform a useful service by removing the dung from the soil surface and hastening its breakdown in the soil.

The Egyptians called scarab beetles "Khepera." The god Kheper, or Khepri, represents spontaneous creation, regeneration, new life, virility, and resurrection, an earthly symbol of the life-giving sun. Kheper says, "I developed myself from the primeval matter which I made, I developed myself out of the primeval matter," signifying that the descent under the earth into the tomb was only a prologue to rebirth and endless life in a continual cycle.

Since locks were unknown, important documents and the contents of jars, bags, boxes, and storage rooms were sealed for protection with a scarab seal bearing the name of the owner. Secular, religious, and governmental organizations all had official seals and sealers. In addition to mummified scarabs found in Egyptian tombs—to ensure eternal resurrection—representations of scarabs appeared in all manner of art. In Karnak today a large scarab statue resides beside the sacred lake in the temple of Amun. A similar granite scarab is on display at the British Museum in London.

Most scarabs were small, however, and were worn or carried as amulets by people of all classes—rich and poor—for luck and protection. They were carved of steatite, a soft soapstone, and glazed in blue-green shades like the wings of the scarab. Other commonly available scarabs were molded in glass or faience, a ceramic material made from crushed quartz, glass, or cloisonné. (Steatite and faience scarabs from earlier times are sometimes available today.) Others were carved in such semiprecious stones as amethyst, carnelian, lapis lazuli, basalt, limestone, malachite, schist, serpentine, turquoise, and alabaster. Some were even made of gold or silver, but few of these remain. The undersides of the abdomens were carved with geometric designs, hieroglyphic names of pharaohs, and magical inscriptions. After the scarab was fabricated, it was sanctified in an elaborate rite called the "ceremony of the beetle," which could only be efficaciously performed on nine sacred days of the month.

Scarabs were made into bracelets and rings, carved into beads, and strung with gold wire into necklaces, pendants, and pectorals. There were special scarabs to bring luck in marriage, to avert evil during childbirth, to guarantee success for lion hunts, and to commemorate special dates or events. Larger ones, known as heart scarabs and made of green material—ideally green jasper—were placed on the throat, neck, or heart of the mummified bodies of the deceased, or sewn into the wrappings. The earliest examples of heart scarabs are from the Hyksos Period, Dynasty XVII. Some heart scarabs showed the wings outstretched to provide a safe journey into the Afterworld. Heart scarabs often bear an inscribed spell, in the form of a prayer, that there would be no hindrance before the divine court of judgment, that the deceased's heart would not weigh too much on the Scales of Truth.

Today—four thousand years later—Pagans, especially Kemetic Pagans, wear images of scarabs near the heart or elsewhere for luck and protection, just as ancient Egyptians did.

12

The *Epic of Gilgamesh*

Mythologists, and many Pagans, have long been fascinated by the lengthy and complex *Epic of Gilgamesh*, believed to be an assemblage of several tales told among the peoples of the ancient Near East. Versions of the story were told in Sumerian, Babylonian, Assyrian, Akkadian, and Hittite. It dates from around 2750 to 2500 B.C.E., and was committed to cuneiform writing in Sumerian on twelve clay tablets. The central character, Gilgamesh, is ruler of Uruk (sometimes spelled Erech) from which Iraq, the present name for that region, is derived. He is believed to have been two-thirds god and one-third human. Gilgamesh, like many strong men who come into power at a young age, is a tyrant to the people of Uruk. He oppresses his people, who called upon the gods for help. Their pleas

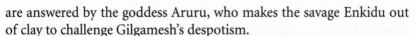

are answered by the goddess Aruru, who makes the savage Enkidu out of clay to challenge Gilgamesh's despotism.

Enkidu lives in the wilderness surrounding Gilgamesh's lands, until a trapper discovers him running naked with the animals of the forests. When the trapper reports this to his father, his father urges him to go into the city to fetch one of the temple harlots to seduce Enkidu. The harlot Shamhat finds Enkidu and offers herself to him. The peril to Enkidu of accepting her offer is that he will lose his strength and wildness. In return, however, he will gain understanding and knowledge. Enkidu laments his lost state. First he lives with a group of shepherds who gradually teach him to wear clothing, speak properly, and tend flock. Then Shamhat the harlot takes him to the city to enjoy the joys of civilization. There she introduces him to Gilgamesh.

Meanwhile, Gilgamesh is claiming his right as king to sexual intercourse with every new bride on her wedding day. The simpler Enkidu takes great offense at this practice, so he blocks Gilgamesh's entry into the bridal chamber. This results in a furious fight between the two men, with Gilgamesh eventually gaining the upper hand. Enkidu concedes, they embrace, and thereafter become devoted friends.

Gilgamesh and Enkidu enjoy each other's company but begin to weaken and grow lazy with city life. So Gilgamesh proposes that the two travel to the great Cedar Forest (in either Lebanon or Persia, depending on the version of the story) to cut down all the cedar trees. This forest is guarded by a demon called Humbaba the Terrible. Reluctantly agreeing, the elders of Uruk insist that Enkidu take the forward position to protect their ruler in the coming battle with Humbaba. The sun god Shamash promises Gilgamesh's mother that he will ensure Gilgamesh's safety. Enkidu tries to dissuade Gilgamesh because he knows Humbaba from his days in the wilderness.

The two companions journey for six days to reach the Cedar Forest, during which time Gilgamesh prays to Shamash and receives a series of oracular dreams. These dreams assure Gilgamesh that Shamash will keep him from harm, but even so, when they approach the entrance both Gilgamesh and Enkidu lose courage for the impending encounter. They argue and fall upon each other. Then they begin to cut down trees. Humbaba, aroused by the ruckus, emerges and challenges them. At the end of the ensuing battle between Gilgamesh and Humbaba, Gilgamesh decapitates Humbaba with his mighty sword, but not before Humbaba curses Enkidu, saying, "Of the two of you, may Enkidu not live the longer, may Enkidu not find any peace in this world!" The two victors cut down the forest, load up a raft, and float down the Euphrates to Uruk, taking the tallest trees to make the great cedar gate for the city.

Gilgamesh's fame spreads after these escapades, and the alluring goddess Ishtar, attracted by his strength and status, attempts to seduce Gilgamesh. She says, "Come, Gilgamesh, be my lover! Give me the taste of your body." Gilgamesh rudely refuses her offers, saying, "You are a cooking fire that goes out in the cold, a back door that keeps out neither wind nor storm, a palace that crushes the brave ones defending it, a well whose lid collapses, pitch that dirties one who is carrying it, a waterksin that soaks the one who lifts it, limestone that crumbles in the stone wall, a battering-ram that shatters in the land of the enemy, a shoe that pinches the owner's foot!"

Ishtar pleads with her father, the sky-god Anu, to give her the mighty Bull of Heaven to avenge the insult. Indeed, its breathing is so powerful that it causes the opening of enormous abysses in the earth. Hundreds of people fall to their death in the abysses. Gilgamesh and Enkidu team up again and together they slay the bull. Nevertheless, Humbaba's curse has yet to be realized. The chief gods meet and decide that the killing of Humbaba and the Bull of Heaven must be avenged. Of the two men, the gods choose Enkidu for punishment. They cause Enkidu to take ill.

Enkidu curses the injustice of this decision. He defames the trapper for introducing him to civilization, the harlot Shamhat, and the great Cedar Gate of the city. Shamash, however, reminds him of the pleasures and happiness he has enjoyed. Enkidu then blesses Shamhat and the trapper. Enkidu lingers, during which time he dreams of being taken to the House of Dust, "the house where the dead . . . drink dirt and eat stone . . . where no light ever invades their everlasting darkness, where the door and the lock of Hell is coated with thick dust . . . there sat Erishkigal, the queen. . . ." After twelve days of suffering and pain, Enkidu dies.

Gilgamesh laments. He neglects to bathe and shave and change his clothes. He decides to travel to Utnapishtim, survivor of the Great Flood, in his home on Mount Mashu to seek his secret of eternal life. Gilgamesh travels through the land of Night for twelve leagues before finally reaching a brilliant garden of gems, where every tree bears precious stones. He arrives at a tavern by the ocean, where he engages Urshanabi, the ferryman, to take him across the Waters of Death to Utnapishtim.

Utnapishtim tells Gilgamesh that he can gain the gift of immortality if he can stay awake for six days and seven nights. Gilgamesh accepts and then goes right to sleep. Utnapishtim tells his wife that all men are liars, that Gilgamesh will deny having fallen asleep. He then asks his wife to bake a loaf of bread every day that Gilgamesh remains asleep. After six days and seven nights, Utnapishtim awakens the king, whereupon the startled Gilgamesh says, "I only just dozed off for half a second here." A distraught Gilgamesh views the proof in the stale loaves of bread.

Regardless, Utnapishtim tells Gilgamesh of a secret plant that grows at the bottom of the ocean surrounding the Far-Away that can give immortality. Gilgamesh ties stones to his feet and descends to the depths to pick the magic plant. But just to be sure it works, Gilgamesh decides to take the plant back to Uruk and test it on an old man first. On their way back, Gilgamesh and Urshanabi stop to rest. While they sleep, a snake eats the plant and crawls away. This is why snakes shed their skin. The tale ends with Gilgamesh showing the ferryman the splendid gates of Uruk.

In 1993, archaeologists in Iraq found what they believe might be the lost tomb of King Gilgamesh.

13

Gundestrup Cauldron

The Gundestrup Cauldron, dating just after 120 B.C.E. and now housed in the National Museum in Copenhagen, is fourteen inches high, weighs nearly twenty pounds, and is made of thirteen individual richly decorated silver plates. When it was reassembled, it was found to have a capacity of 28.5 gallons of liquid. It was unearthed from a bog in Gundestrup, Denmark, in 1880. Originally the cauldron was gilt with gold leaf, the silver object having been made with Persian coins, most likely by Scythian silversmiths, who lived in present-day Ukraine. Whatever its exact origins, it is considered one of the greatest treasures of Celtic silver art.

Some of the figures on the Gundestrup Cauldron are believed to be Celtic deities, including images tentatively identified as Teutates, meaning "god of the tribe," and Cernunnos, an antlered god. There is a goddess figure that some believe is similar to imagery associated with the Irish Medb, a goddess of mead, prophecy, and intoxication. There are four male and three female deific figures depicted on the seven outer plates of the cauldron.

Bulls, wolves, lions, birds, and stags are also portrayed on the plates, as is an elephant and a pair of leopards. Other exotic, unidentifiable animals include creatures that might be gryphons—the mythic creatures with bodies of lions and the heads, wings, and claws of eagles. There is a boy riding a dolphin on one panel as well. Ram-horned snakes are shown, too; this creature is found on at least thirty different monuments and figurines from Gaul and Britain. One plate bears the image of warriors carrying a tree in procession, and a deity holding a smaller human figure head-first over a cauldron. Cauldrons have long been associated with healing, wisdom, plenty, magic, and the gods in Celtic mythology. Many Celtic deities, such as the Irish god the Dagda and the Welsh goddess Cerridwen, owned magical cauldrons possessing powers of regeneration. In Ireland the *Filidh*, or sacred poets, taught that people had three cauldrons within themselves that provided and processed their personal power and wisdom.

Some suggest that what the warriors are carrying is the Celtic tree of life, called a *bile* in Ireland. These sacred trees were believed to be the homes of gods and spirits, and kings were inaugurated under them. The king's staff was made from the bile that was associated with him, and a branch of his tree was symbolic of his rank. Each of Ireland's five provinces had its own sacred tree, and each of these trees might be a different species.

The figure held by a deity over the cauldron is probably an illustration of a sacrificial ritual. Though we can never know for certain what the original artists intended to depict, the art itself is surprisingly beautiful and mysterious. It delights the modern eye and draws us to contemplate the possibilities of the myth inherent in the story or stories these images are intended to convey.

Such ancient works of sacred art can inspire us to create our own works of beauty for altars and shrines. Many modern Pagan artisans and craft workers work to reproduce early deific icons for modern use. The cup of wine of life, the Holy Grail, and the Witch's cauldron continue to offer purification, healing, and inspiration.

See **Sacred Salmon of Wisdom, Brewing.**

14

Harp and Lyre

Although associated with Greek culture, the lyre didn't originate in Greece. It seems to have entered Greek culture from the orient through Thrace or Lydia. Greeks took to the lyre, making it their own. The Ionian and Aeolian colonies bordered the Lydian empire, and it was these peoples who improved the lyre and adopted it for use in Greek poetry, with which the lyre is so strongly associated. In addition to writing the words they spoke, Greek poets also composed the music to accompany their lyrical recitations.

In Greek legend, it is Orpheus who is known to be master of song, music, and the lyre. His artistry was so compelling that he was said to have been able to charm wild beasts, change the course of rivers, and cause rocks and trees to move from their places. As one of the hero Jason's companions on his expedition aboard the *Argonaut*, Orpheus saved the crew from the deadly Sirens with the beauty of his song. This man, said to be son of the muse Calliope by the king of Thrace, traveled widely. In addition to being a bard, Orpheus, the "father of all songs" was a seer and he practiced astrology.

The lyre and its cousin the harp can be found throughout ancient Greek art painted on pottery, carved into temples, and frescoed on walls. Sometimes the words "lyre" and "harp" are used interchangeably, but they are not the same instrument.

There were two main varieties of lyre: the *kithara* and the *lyra*. Professional musicians such as Sappho played the kithara, a box with symmetrical hollow arms and gut strings which was plucked with a plectrum, or pick. Box lyres were known in Sumeria as far back as 2800 B.C.E. Cretan frescoes dating from 1450 B.C.E. show people playing these lyres. The *kinnor* played by the ancient Hebrew King David was similar to the kithara.

The lyra, typically made of tortoise shell with a belly of bull's hide, was a bowl rather than a box. Amateurs played lyras by plucking the gut strings with their fingers. Today East Africans continue to play the *beganna* and Ethiopians the *krar*, both of which are types of lyra.

The oldest harps, known in both Sumer and Egypt as long ago as 3000 to 2000 B.C.E., had an arched shape. Angular harps followed. This ancient type of harp is still in use today in Myanmar (formerly Burma), and parts of Afghanistan, Africa, and Siberia. The well-known Irish harp is a frame harp, consisting of a large sound box from which the sounds emanate. The Irish harp, hewn from a single block of wood and strung with thirty to fifty brass strings, wasn't developed until the ninth century C.E. in Europe.

Another harp, the Aeolian harp, differs from others in that it is not played by a person but rather by the wind. Aeolus, the god of the winds, was thought to inspirit the instrument with his breath. The Latin word *spiritus* means both breath and wind. Aeolian harps are still heard today, their eerie tones made louder and softer with the changes in wind intensity.

The stringing of ancient lyres with from three to eight strings varied by locality and in different epochs. More strings enabled the player to produce ever more complex music. Thanks to our Pagan ancestors, harp music continues to sound in praise of the divine and to bring pleasure to our ears.

See **Enheduanna, Mercury/Hermes, Sappho.**

15

The *Iliad*

The Greek poet Homer is thought to have composed The *Iliad* around 850 B.C.E. The *Iliad* tells of the events preceding Odysseus's journey to the Trojan War. His other epic, The *Odyssey*, tells of the adventures of one of the Greek warriors, Odysseus, after the war's end. So resonant are these tales that even today we speak of "the face that launched a thousand ships," "the golden apple," "the apple of his eye," and "beware of Greeks bearing gifts."

The face, of course, is that of Helen, winner of a divine beauty contest which set the entire series of events that comprise the poem in motion—and does indeed launch a thousand ships. Helen's brother-in-law, Agamemnon ("very resolute"), had entered one of Artemis's sacred groves and killed one of her sacred deer, and afterward boasted that he was a better hunter than the goddess. Artemis punishes Agamemnon for this arrogant presumption by stilling the winds near Aulis and preventing him from leaving to lay siege to Troy. The oracle Calchas—oracles figure prominently throughout the war and its aftermath—tells the king that in order to gain a favorable wind, he must sacrifice his daughter Iphigenia. In one version of the story, he does so, but in another he sacrifices a deer. In any case, after a sacrifice, the winds stir and he goes on to battle and glory.

This precedes the famous event that started the trouble—the Judgment of Paris. The gods hold a great wedding feast at Olympus for the marriage of Peleus and Thetis, who would become the parents of the hero Achilles. However, wishing to avoid trouble, they snub Eris ("chaos"), goddess of strife. One cannot offend a goddess, though, without repercussions. Eris thus tosses a golden apple into the festivities. The apple is inscribed "Kallisti"—"For the most beautiful one." As expected, this strikes the vanity of the other Olympian goddesses, causing them to quarrel over who deserves the apple. The Trojan prince, Paris, is chosen to judge. Hera, Athena, and Aphrodite try to bribe Paris with promises of political power, wisdom and skill in battle, and the prize of the most beautiful woman in the world, respectively. (Perhaps this is the origin of our modern beauty pageants.)

Like many young men, Paris follows his loins rather than his mind. Or perhaps he falls in love? In any case, he gives the golden apple to Aphrodite. In return the goddess gives him Helen, the most beautiful woman in the world, to be his wife, no matter that she is already married to the Spartan—Menelaus. There are, of course, other more political reasons for the Achaeans (the Greeks around the Aegean Sea) to want to conquer Troy. Troy, known as Ilium, is a wealthy city strategically located near the Dardanelles Strait in what is present-day Turkey.

The Achaeans could gain a distinct commercial and strategic advantage if they could control the Dardanelles.

Homer, writing his poem centuries after the war circa 1200 B.C.E., sings only of the last year of a draining ten-year siege in the *Iliad*, during which time the attackers had fought battle after battle with the Trojan soldiers on the seaward plains outside the walls of the city. It tells of the Greek warrior Achilles, his love for his friend Patroclus, and his revenge against Patroclus's killer, the Trojan prince Hector. In his grief, Achilles kills Hector and inflicts the added cruel humiliation of dragging his body from the back of his chariot three times around before relinquishing it to Hector's family for a proper burial.

The tales are filled with interventions by the gods and dire oracular predictions: Because Achilles' mother, the sea nymph Thetis, cast a spell of protection on him when he was a baby, Achilles cannot be wounded anywhere but in his heel, or "Achilles tendon." Aeneas's mother, Aphrodite, protects her son when he is in danger by hiding him in a cloud conjured by Apollo. The seer Calchas counsels Agamemnon; the Trojan oracle Helenus, son of King Priam, is tortured by the attackers to learn how Troy can be taken. Thetis persuades the smith god Hephaestus to make new armor for Achilles. An oracle told Greeks to bring along the bones of a man named Pelops, ruler of most of Peloponnesus and bearer of a curse upon his descendants (Atreus, Agamemnon, Menelaus, and Orestes among them), or they could not win.

But most memorable, both Cassandra, daughter of King Priam and Queen Hecuba, sister of Hector of Troy, and the blind Laocoon are seers who speak against receiving the gift of a horse that the Greeks want to give Troy as a peace offering. This "gift borne by Greeks," which is hollow and filled with Greek soldiers, allows the Greeks entry to the city. Once inside, they wait until the Trojans are sated with celebration, then emerge from the horse, open the gates to the warriors waiting outside, and sack the city.

The aftermath of all this is violence. These fascinating stories about our Pagan ancestors have inspired artists ever since. Euripides, Chaucer, Berlioz, and many painters, sculptors, writers, and composers—all have been captivated.

See **Aphrodite, Artemis, Oracles and Seers, The** *Odyssey,* **Homer.**

16

The *Kalevala*

The *Kalevala* is a collection of thirty-two cantos compiled by Elias Lönnrot in the nineteenth century from the oral poetry he compiled and recorded of unschooled people in the rural areas of northeastern Finland and part of the Karelian-speaking Russian Province of Archangel.

Karelian is a language similar to Finnish. At that time, Swedish was the official language of Finland, and young Finnish intellectuals sought to help create a distinctive cultural identity rooted in the language and oral literature of the ordinary people. One result of this movement was the acceptance, in the 1860s, of Finnish as one of two (with Swedish) of Finland's official languages of education, administration, and government.

Over time, the *Kalevala* has become the most translated work of Finnish literature. It served as a source of inspiration, context, and substance for Finnish artists, musicians, writers, designers, and architects during the Golden Age of Finnish Art, roughly from 1890 to 1910, when the arts also were flourishing in Ireland and many other parts of Europe. The music of the famous Finnish composer Sibelius helped bring the *Kalevala* to the consciousness of the wider intellectual and artistic world.

These stories speak of heroes and magic workers, the primeval world and creation, gods, and spirits. They arise within peoples who are intimately connected with Nature. A host of unseen forces affect their world. The people's well-being depends upon the harmonious functioning of the sun and the moon, plants, animals, mountains, and streams. The primary character in the *Kalevala* tales, for example, is Väinämöinen, a sage and magician, one of those who attempts to summon help from the Otherworld. Elsewhere in the epic, magic-workers ward off disease and heal the sick; they protect livestock and travelers with spells and incantations.

The poetry that Lönnrot collected was sung in an unusual, highly formalized, archaic trochaic tetrameter that had been part of the oral tradition of Balto-Finnic language speakers for two thousand years. Interestingly, American poet Longfellow imitated this ancient form in his "Song of Hiawatha." To begin the recitation of the stories, the singers sit hand to hand. In this way they can support each other for many hours of storytelling.

Early in the series, Väinämöinen meets up with another hero, a Saami singer and magician named Joukkahainen. They take to fighting, Väinämöinen wins, and Joukkahainen promises his sister, Aino, in marriage to Väinämöinen. Aino wants none of it. Rather than marry the old magician, she drowns herself in the sea, where her blood is transformed into water, her ribs into willows, her flesh into fish, and her hair into sea grass.

Upon the advice of his mother, Väinämöinen travels north to seek another bride. He faces a series of wondrous, if harrowing, adventures—losing his horse, being borne far away by a mighty storm, swimming six days and six nights (or for eight years) through the sea, being rescued by an eagle and taken to the Northland. A later tale tells of a magical Sampo, or mill, crafted by Ilmarinen, a master smith and brother of Väinämöinen. The Sampo could grind out a never-ending supply of riches and food for whomever owned it. There is dispute between old Väinämöinen, Ilmarinen (another younger hero), Lemminkäinen, and the ruler of the North, Old Louhi, about the ownership of this wondrous mill, until it falls into the sea and breaks up. But even its fragments are magical. Väinämöinen gathers pieces from the surface of the sea and takes them home, where they cause the land to be "rich in barley and the flowing ale that is brewed of the barley grain, and rich in rye and the crusty bread that is made of the rye flour."

These few paragraphs are just a sample from among the many marvelous tales of old Väinämöinen and his companions that are told by the sacred singers of Finland.

17

Masks

Men wearing animal masks are painted on the walls of the cave in southern France called "the sorcerer," in Cave of Les Trois Frères in Ariège, France; this cave was occupied by prehistoric peoples. We surmise that these masks had a magical purpose of identifying the hunter with his prey. They helped the hunter align his spirit with that of the game, allowed him to better track the herd, and gave him courage.

Since the invention of agriculture, masks have been used in fertility rituals for crops. The Iroquois of North America used corn husk masks in harvest rituals to give thanks and to ensure future fertility. Perhaps

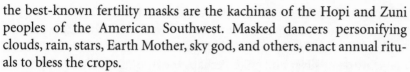

the best-known fertility masks are the kachinas of the Hopi and Zuni peoples of the American Southwest. Masked dancers personifying clouds, rain, stars, Earth Mother, sky god, and others, enact annual rituals to bless the crops.

Masks become suffused with the great supernatural or spirit power. The mask enables the wearer to lose his or her previous identity and assume a new one. Wearing the mask puts the wearer in direct association with the spirit force of the mask. Sometimes the mask wearer undergoes a psychic change or becomes entranced, and assumes the spirit character depicted by the mask. This change is magically enhanced when the wearer, often accompanied by music, drumming, cymbals, or other sounds, dances and postures in attunement with the image of the mask. Masks are a means of contacting various spirit powers, including the spirits of the materials of which the mask is made. Materials can include wood, metal, shells, fiber, ivory, clay, horn, stone, leather, furs, feathers, bark, grasses, flowers, or cloth. Masks are also used as a means of contacting ancestors to act as intermediaries for transmission of petitions or offerings of respect to the gods.

Some masks are portraits of a specific person, such as in the case of a funeral or burial mask. Ancient Romans, for example, crafted waxen masks resembling the deceased; these masks were placed on the face of the dead person or worn by an actor hired to accompany a funeral cortege to the burial site. Mycenaean tombs dating from around 1400 B.C.E. contained beaten gold portrait masks. Cambodian and Siamese (Thai) people put gold masks on their dead, and ancient Incas put gold masks on mummies. Egyptians from Middle Kingdom (circa 2040–1786 B.C.E.) to the first century C.E. covered the faces of their dead with simple painted masks. Rulers and other people of high status in that society had burial masks made of silver and gold. Perhaps the most splendid example was made of gold around 1350 B.C.E. for the pharaoh Tutankhamen. In many cultures, both in the past and today, there is a high priest or priestess, medicine person or shaman, who has his or her own powerful totem (power animal or animal ally). The shaman wears a sacred mask connecting her or him to the totem in order to do the work of exorcising evil spirits, punishing enemies, locating game or fish, predicting or influencing weather, and curing diseases and healing. Chinese children wore protective masks against measles. In China and Burma people wore masks during cholera epidemics.

In some cultures judges wore masks for anonymity and to prevent retribution. Ancient Greeks and Romans painted grotesque masks on their armor or shields for courage and ferocity. Roman horsemen mounted masks on their helmets. From 600 B.C.E., Egyptians used animal masks to illustrate religious beliefs by assuming the characters in sacred stories. Later, in fifth-century B.C.E. Greece, in the earliest theater, a narrator used a different mask to represent each different character. Greek theater emerged from the worship of Dionysus, in which communicants impersonated the deity by wearing goatskins and drinking wine.

Actors in early Greek theater wore outsized masks of leather or canvas painted with exaggerated features and incorporated with a megaphone to project the actor's voice and depict the personalities, ages, ranks, occupations, and moods of each character. Actually, the Greek word for actor is *hypocrites*, leading to our English word "hypocrite" (meaning two-faced), which isn't so surprising as narrator(s) in Greek plays changed masks so they could represent many characters.

Tibetan sacred dramas are performed in masks of papier mâché, cloth and gilt copper, embodying demons and deities in mystery plays. In the lion and dragon dances of China and Japan, the mask is carried on a pole, followed by a troupe under the body of a beast. The head is violently manipulated, and loud clacking sounds are made with its movable jaw, accompanied by dancing, drums, and firecrackers. The spirit of the lion or dragon protects the people from malevolence and brings them health and prosperity.

Individual clans make masks to house the totem spirit of the clan, usually an animal. These totem ancestor masks are worn by elders in nocturnal initiatory rites; they consolidate family pride and distinguish social lines. Masks may be inherited within families, clans, or special societies, or they may be passed from individual to individual. Repainting and redecorating are means for younger members to spiritually reactivate the masks.

Many Pagans today make their own magical masks and use them for similar purposes—reenacting sacred drama, contacting ancestors and the divine, allying with totem animals—as our ancestors all over the world used them.

See **Theater.**

18

Morris Dancing

It seems probable that Morris Dancing is a remnant of ancient pre-Christian Celtic, or Druidic, pagan fertility rites, perhaps performed in stone circles or other megalithic monuments and sacred sites.

Morris Dance is more ritual dance than social dance. It is done in sets of four, six, or eight dancers. Some Morris Dance teams are all men, but most are mixed gender, especially in the United States today. Costumes vary by team, or "set," with different colors to differentiate them. Most, but not all, costumes consist of a white shirt and trousers, with a colored waistcoat, or colored sashes or baldrics (belt extending from shoulder to opposite hip) worn over one or both shoulders. Dancers wear bells strapped around their legs, and often ribbons and flowers. They dance with sticks, which they clash together in formal patterns with great gusto. Sometimes they dance with swords or even antlers, as in the Abbot's Bromley. Dancers take their dancing seriously. Each set or village has its own steps and dances. The dances have magic power and serve both to bring luck and to ward off evil. The ringing of the dancers' bells and the fluttering of their handkerchiefs attract beneficial influence, while the loud, vigorous clashing of sticks scare off malevolent spirits.

There are many theories as to the origin of the word "morris." None is certain, but a reasonable theory is that morris is a corruption of "moorish"—boggy land, moorland, heathland. It was the peasantry, the people of the land, the pagans, who lived on the heaths.

The Morris Dance has general connections with other ritual folk dances, such as the *santiagos, moriscas* (a possible source of the word morris), and *matachinas* of the Mediterranean and Latin America, as well as the *calusara* of Romania. Geoffrey of Monmouth, writing in the twelfth century of the Common Era, describes such a dance having been performed at Stonehenge, which he called the Dance of the Giants (*chorea gigantum*). Shakespeare, in *All's Well That Ends Well,* speaks of Morris Dancing on May Day and it is associated with Beltaine in our day as well.

Today, Morris Dances are done in the open air of rural English villages, in little towns in Massachusetts, and in the coastal hills of California—even in plazas and transit stations in big cities. Although the ultimate source of Morris Dancing remains hidden, its performance can be seen today at NeoPagan celebrations worldwide.

See **Carnac, May Day, Stonehenge.**

19

Mother Goddess Motifs

Folk costumes and household articles throughout the world are decorated with a surprisingly narrow range of motifs. And most have strong Pagan origins. Today, very few who carefully add these decorative designs to their clothing, household linens, furniture, and pottery are aware of the deep Pagan significance of these images. But from Bulgaria to Brazil, from vases of ancient Greece to the glittering wedding costumes of Norwegian brides, artisans—albeit frequently unconsciously—are continually bringing pre-Christian deities back to life. Almost every culture with a textile tradition has images of the "tree of life," the sun, animals with horns, and female figures with upraised hands. Most frequently these images are worked in red, the color of life, the color of blood.

By far the most common motif is the tree-of-life design, typically a symmetrical tree rising from a vase, an urn, or even a heart shape. Trees of life show up on Egyptian pottery, Pennsylvania Dutch wedding chests, English schoolgirls' samplers, Turkish wall hangings, Mexican clay candelabra, Scandinavian ski sweaters, and pieced Baltimore-album quilts. Frequently the tree is hung with pomegranates that are themselves symbols of the fertile womb of the great mother goddess. The fruitfulness of the tree is a reference to the divinely given abundance of Nature. And the fact that trees have their roots in the earth and their branches in the air symbolized the three spheres of existence: the past, the present, and the future.

Many circular designs are references to the sun as divinity and source of all life. Solar motifs are hidden in the rosette patterns in embroidery on Hungarian blouses; they show up in Uzbekistan's Suzani wall hangings appliquéd with large silk circles, they are engraved on Bronze Age razors found in Germany, and they are found in the embroidery motifs on Berber women's shawls from western Egypt. Neolithic pottery in Romania features circular sun-wheel motifs as do Iberian cave paintings. The sun assumes a diamond shape in both the weavings of the indigenous people of Guatemala and the paintings executed with a mixture of chewed alder bark and saliva on the oval shamanic drums of the Saami people of northern Scandinavia.

Deer are another common folk-art motif. Deer are the embodiment of wild animal spirits and are associated with the goddess Artemis in the Greek pantheon. The many-branched antlers of the deer are often stylized in folk embroidery as a tree of life: the fact that deer grow and shed antlers in the course of a year is seen as a symbol of life and rebirth. Deer motifs are practically ubiquitous, with representations ranging from cave art to samplers to knitting patterns. Frequently the deer are shown with lowered head drinking the water of life that flows from beneath the world tree.

Many Pagans are relearning the crafts of their ancestors, and they are quick to pick up and use these familiar motifs. However, these days Pagans are as likely to work a sun-wheel design in Fimo clay or sew a tree-of-life banner from Ripstop nylon as they would be to knit, weave, or embroider these designs. And at warm-weather Pagan gatherings, it's possible to see another favorite use of these ancient motifs. Today many Pagans take their ancestors' folk-art designs closely to heart, with sun wheels, trees of life, deer, and many other traditional designs showing up as tattoos on virtually any body part. The tattoos are for much more than mere decoration. In most cases, Pagans will choose to get a tattoo to mark a significant life event or to bring a symbol of power or ancestral roots to their own bodies.

See **Art, Pottery, Linen, Marija Gimbutas, Artemis, Demeter and Persephone/Kore, Yggdrassil.**

20

The *Odyssey*

The great composer of Greek epic poetry, Homer, wrote two major works about the Trojan War and its aftermath. The first is the *Iliad*; the *Odyssey* is his second. It concerns Odysseus, the king of Ithaca, who reluctantly left to join Agamemnon and his Mycenaean colleagues in their ten-year siege of Troy, and his long, adventure-filled return home to his wife, Penelope.

To assist Odysseus (or, as the Romans called him, Ulysses) on his journey home after the Aechaeans conquered Troy, Aeolus—god of the winds—gives him a bag containing each of the four winds. Unfortunately, one of his crew opens the bag when they are nearly home, and they are blown back to the beginning of their trip. After much hardship, including no winds for their sails, Odysseus and his men land on what is believed to be the shores of Libya, where they encounter the natives eating lotus flowers. The crew, too, partake of the flowers, which causes them to sink into apathy and forget about going home. Odysseus, neverthe-

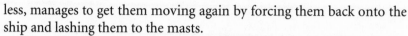

less, manages to get them moving again by forcing them back onto the ship and lashing them to the masts.

In another port, this time on the island of the Cyclopes (Sicily), Odysseus and his scouting party venture into a large cave, where they proceed to feast on the food they find there. They are unaware, however, that the cave is the home of the one-eyed monster Polyphemus. Upon finding his stores pillaged, the Cyclopes attacks, eating several of the men. Odysseus manages to get Polyphemus drunk on unwatered wine, and when the giant falls asleep, Odysseus and his men pierce his eye with a spear and blind the monster. Then they tie themselves under the bellies of Polyphemus's sheep so that when the blind monster lets his sheep out to graze, the men are able to escape. Odysseus doesn't know, however, that Polyphemus is the son of the sea-god Poseidon, and this act earns Odysseus Poseidon's enmity.

The next stop for the lost Greeks is the island of the enchantress Circe. At a feast she gives in their honor, Circe drugs the men with one of her magical potions and turns them all into pigs. Odysseus and his suspicious friend, Eurylochus, however, have remained aboard the ship. When he sets out to rescue his comrades, Odysseus takes an herb given him by the god Hermes to counteract Circe's magic. Ultimately, Odysseus is able to leave Circe's island, but not before siring three children with her (some sources say four). One of the sons of that union, Telegonus, will be responsible for his father's death many years later.

Odysseus then seeks the counsel of his dead friend Achilles in the

Underworld, after obtaining permission from its ruler, Hades. There he receives valuable advice on how to finish his journey and arrive safely in Ithaca. Among the subsequent challenges Odysseus and his crew face include when they eat the sacred cattle of the daughters of the sun god Helios, which so angers the god he destroys their ship. They negotiate the treacherous whirlpools of the monsters Scylla and Charybdis ("sucker down"), a maneuver that results in the sacrifice of some of the crew. They also succeed in passing the dangerously alluring Sirens: Odysseus plugs the crew's ears with wax and has himself tied to the mast until they are safely beyond the range of hearing the Sirens' song. They also escape the cannibalistic Antiphates, and eventually encounter Calypso.

Calypso is a nymph who falls in love with Odysseus and keeps him with her for seven years with the promise of immortality. Eventually, Hermes intervenes on behalf of the other Olympians, except Poseidon, and persuades Calypso to release Odysseus. The Ithacans endure two more shipwrecks before, with the help of the Phaeacian princess Nausicaa, they return home.

Odysseus arrives home to find Penelope fending off suitors. She had said that when she is done weaving a burial shroud for Odysseus she will remarry, but she unravels her work every night. Odysseus, in disguise, then kills the suitors who had been abusing his family's hospitality and is reunited with his faithful wife.

Odysseus himself is accidently killed by his son by Circe, Telegonus, with the spine of a stingray, when the latter attacks Ithaca, mistakes it for the city Corcyra. The tales of dangerous enchantresses, natural perils such as whirlpools, and the patience of Penelope are familiar themes many centuries after they were first told. Some even refer to long, complicated journeys as being their own odysseys.

See **The** *Iliad,* **The** *Aenead,* **Homer, Cumaean Sybil.**

21

Prehistoric "Venus" Figurines

Round and sensual, ancient small carvings of nude or nearly nude female figures have been found in many places throughout Europe. They are small and portable, fitting easily in the hand. Made of limestone, steatite, calcite, jet, or mammoth ivory, most are named for the places where they were found. For example, the Venus of Monpazier has protuberant breasts, belly, and buttocks and a well-drawn vulva. She's made of shiny green steatite. Another, the Dolni Vestonice, is a statuette of a woman found in Czechia and made of burnt soil. From Dordogne, France, the headless Venus de Sireil is made of a pinkish translucent calcite. A calcite figure, the Venus de Tursac, dates from 20,000 B.C.E.

The Savignano Venus, from the north Italian plain, is made of serpentine. She is long and tapered, with an indication of arms across her breasts.

One of the most remarkable Venuses comes from the excavation of a habitation of Paleolithic (Old Stone Age) hunters near Stratzing, Austria. Called Venus vom Galgenberg, she is the oldest figure of a woman, aside from the 800,000-year-old Berekhat Ram figure, created around 30,000 B.C.E. She is posed in a dancing attitude, with her upper body turned to the side, her left arm raised, right hand on her thigh, one breast jutting out to the left and the other facing frontward, and with a clearly defined vulva. She's made of shiny, greenish, amphibolite slate.

Arguably the best known of the Venus figures is the Venus of Willendorf, found in Austria. She is made of fine-grained dense limestone with traces of red dye on the surface. Her faceless head is covered with little knobby spirals that look like cornrows. She has enormous breasts and belly, a distinct navel and vulva, short little legs, and small arms crossed over her breasts. Willendorf is $4\frac{3}{8}$ inches high and dates from 24,000–22,000 B.C.E. The Gagarino Venus from the Ukraine is similar in form to Willendorf, although she doesn't have cornrows on her head. Another small figure, made of jet, hard coal that is light and easy to polish, the Venus of Neuchatel, Switzerland, has a hole carved in it, suggesting that it may have been hung as a pendant on a narrow strip of leather. Neuchatel dates from 11,000 B.C.E.

The Lion Lady, Die Lowenfrau, comes from a cave in Germany.

She—or it could be a he—is carved of mammoth ivory, pieced together from two hundred tiny fragments. Years after her initial discovery, her ivory muzzle that fit perfectly was found in the same cave.

One of the most intriguing of the Venus figurines is the Kostenki limestone Venus from Russia. At 5½ inches, she is also the largest of the handheld statuettes by far. Like the others, she has a large belly. Her navel is prominent. Her fingers are articulated and she wears bracelets on her wrists that appear to be joined together at the front like a pair of handcuffs. Her head and legs are missing. Another Venus exists with nearly the same name—the Kostienki Venus. Made of mammoth bone rather than limestone, she, too, has big breasts, belly, and buttocks, and appears to be wearing a girdle. Yet another Kostenki/ Kostenky/ Kostienki Venus, dating from 23,000–21,000 B.C.E., is a faceless image. Rows of incisions on her head indicate a hairstyle or cap. She's carved with a breast ornament tied at the back and bracelets on her wrists

The Venus of Lauselle is one of the few non-portable Venus figures. She was discovered carved into the wall of a limestone rock shelter in the Dordogne near Lauselle, France. Over three hundred yards long, the terrace offers a view of the valley below from under an overhang. It seems to have been a ceremonial site. The Venus of Lauselle has been detached from her original home and now lives in the Musee d'Aquitane in Bordeaux. She dates from 27,000 to 22,000 B.C.E. She has wide hips, pendulous breasts, and a big belly, and in her right hand she holds a bison's horn carved with thirteen lines. These lines may be linked with menstruation; they may represent the thirteen days of the waxing moon or the thirteen months of the lunar year.

These intriguing sculptures suggest a reverence for the female. Perhaps they were intended to represent the great mother, the divine source of all.

See **Art, Calendars, Mother Goddess Motifs, Earth Mother, Terra Mater, Mother Nature, Marija Gimbutas.**

22

Pisanski Eggs

One of the prime icons and symbols of spring, of birth and rebirth and fertility, is the egg. The Slavic peoples of central and eastern Europe and western Asia, and their descendants around the world, have made decorating and sanctifying eggs an art form. The perfect icon of Slavic beliefs in the creation of the universe from an egg, and of the universe as containing everything needed to be whole, decorated eggs were taken out into farmers' fields as the grains were sown, along with a candle that was blessed at *Gromniczny* (February 2), in order to bring life back into the warming soil. Eggs also were buried at the base of fruit trees to make them bear in abundance. Even the water in which boiled eggs are prepared is sacred: it is used to wash in, bless with, pour along the property lines to protect against lightning and thunder and the ravages of weather, and anoint beehives to bring plenty of sweet-tasting honey.

A bowl of decorated eggs was kept in the home at all times to ensure good health and prosperity—and these were never thrown out. If they were broken, they were returned to the Earth by burial in the garden, or given to the *Rusalki* (water nymphs/spirits) in the nearest river or stream. A great symbol of fertility, eggs traditionally bedeck the breads baked for weddings.

The eggs are decorated in several different styles. Boiled eggs are decorated in single colors, usually red, and are called *krashanka*. These eggs are meant to be eaten, or fed to the livestock, and are dyed with materials safe for consumption, such as berries or beets. *Krapanka* are also boiled eggs, but are not meant to be eaten, and are decorated with multicolored dots. *Drapanka* are boiled eggs dyed a single color, then decorated by scratching a design with a pin or small knife tip. *Lystowka* are wrapped in leaves and subjected to a bath of onionskin water, leaving a beautiful relief pattern. Depending on the types of leaves used, these eggs may also be eaten. *Nalepianki* are decorated in *wycinanki* style, which is the application of cut-paper patterns to the outside of the egg, and *wyklejanki* are adorned with glued-on hollow bull rushes and yarn.

The most common and most tedious form of decoration, however, is called *pisanki*, a batik-method coloring using beeswax, commercial or natural material dyes, and raw eggs. (*Pysansky* is the Russian and Ukrainian spelling; *pisanki* is Polish and Slavic.) Boiling the eggs first will not only alter the significance of the icon, but will allow water to seep through and ruin the dye, or will alter the design by adhering to cracks formed in the boiling process. The artist uses a tool called a "kistka," a writing utensil whose point is a small funnel that holds molten wax, to apply the design to the egg. Like batik, the design takes shape by covering the lightest areas with wax, then dipping the egg into the next darker color, continuing until the last color applied is black. After the dying is complete, the artist holds the egg next to, not directly in, a candle flame, which softens the wax enough to rub it off with a soft cloth, revealing the design.

Ages-old rituals passed from *babci* (grandmother) to her family are used for the preparation of the designs. The creation of all types of these decorated eggs is traditionally done after dark, in a quiet spot that allows concentration, meditation, and ritual consciousness. By custom the artist should have made an effort during the day to remain calm and anger-free. A white tablecloth covers the working area, and a candle is set in the middle. Salt and bread, the staple Slavic symbols of the sacred, are set behind the candle. Hundreds of designs have been passed down through the generations, such as these pre-Christian designs: a set of four called "the Princess, the Queen, the Crone, and the Great Goddess";

forty triangles; the Call of Spring; the Universe; Gates; Birds; and Gypsy Roads. Some are unchanging whole-egg patterns, and others smaller motifs that can be combined to convey new and unique intents.

Traditionally, only women and girls decorated eggs. Now many more men are taking up this ritual as a meaningful expression not only of the spring seasonal celebration, but also of any time the beauty and magic of these written charms is desired.

23

Sacred Salmon of Wisdom

The salmon is a fish of great wisdom in Celtic traditions. Images and tales of the sacred salmon of wisdom are found in Gaul, Britain, Wales, Ireland, the Isle of Man, Cornwall, Brittany, and Scotland. In Ireland, a salmon of wisdom named Fintan lived in the Boyne river, while another, named Goll Essa Ruaidh, lived under the falls of Assaroe. A Welsh salmon of wisdom named Llyn Llew lived in the Severn river. This salmon was called the oldest of living things, and it was considered the wisest of forty animals. In the tale of the youth Mabon, this salmon tells the Welsh prince Culhuwch where Mabon, the stolen child-god, was imprisoned.

In the Irish tradition, the salmon of wisdom also lives in the Other-world, in the wells of Nechtan and Segais, at the heads of the seven sacred rivers of Ireland. Over the wells hang nine hazel trees, and the salmon grow wise from eating the nuts. The spots on each salmon's side show how many of the sacred nuts of wisdom they have eaten.

One Irish story about Fionn mac Cumhaill tells how the warrior-poet and seer finds his powers of prophecy. On the banks of the Boyne River, the poet Finneces, believing himself to be the one chosen to receive the gift of the salmon's wisdom, waits for seven years to catch the salmon Fintan. When he finally catches it, a young boy named Demne happens along. Finneces sets Demne to building a fire and cooking the salmon for him. Demne is instructed not to eat any of the salmon, for it is destined for a man named Fionn. Demne dutifully builds the fire and cooks the salmon, but a few drops of the salmon's juice splashes on him and burns his finger. Demne puts his finger in his mouth to cool it, and in doing so receives the wisdom that was intended for another. At this, Finneces names Demne Fionn, because he can see that this boy and not the old poet himself was the Fionn the prophecy had spoken of.

Upon receiving the wisdom of the salmon, Fionn declaims his first poem, "May-day, fair season!" Its perfection was the sign that Fionn's wisdom and prophetic talent are complete. From that day forward, all Fionn has to do is place his thumb in his mouth and bite down, and he receives any knowledge he seeks.

Taliesin, a Welsh poet associated with the sacred wisdom tradition, flees the goddess Cerridwen's cauldron when he, like the young Fionn, receives the three drops of wisdom on his burned thumb. As he runs, he shifts shape, turning into animals, and finally into a grain. One of his transformations is into a salmon, and Cerridwen becomes an otter to pursue him. When he becomes a grain to hide from her, she becomes a hen and consumes him, later giving birth to him.

Unable to kill him in revenge for receiving the wisdom she intended for her son, Cerridwen ties him in a bag and throws him into the sea. Forty years later, Taliesin is pulled from the bag where it had been trapped in a salmon weir. Upon first seeing the light, Taliesin, like Fionn, sings a poem that demonstrates and confirms his poetic and prophetic knowledge.

These mystic images link our spiritual traditions with the precious salmon in our oceans and rivers. If we wish to learn from the salmon, if we pay attention to Nature as the Celtic ancestors did, we must first preserve them and ensure their survival for future generations.

More and more salmon runs become extinct every year from runoff pollution into rivers and spawning streams, overfishing in the oceans, the drowning of spawning streams by damming, and by silting of spawning beds due to erosion from logging or the improper application of agriculture. We can help, though, by working to restore salmon streams, supporting environmental protection legislation, and fighting to eliminate pollution sources in our homes and local communities.

See **Gundestrup Cauldron.**

24

Spiral Dance

The spiral is found everywhere in Nature. In every culture, past and present, it is a symbol of eternal life. When we look into the heavens on a clear night, we can see the spiraling veil of the Milky Way, the very galaxy of which our green planet Earth and we ourselves are a part. We can sense our connectedness with the multiverse. Closer to home, we see whirlpools in the seas. Whirlpools are such a powerful natural phenomenon that our Pagan ancestors ascribed names and personalities to them, albeit monstrous rather than human ones. The Straits of Messina near Sicily are inhabited by Scylla, who has the face and torso of a woman, but from whose flanks grow six dog heads. Below this her body sprouts twelve canine legs and a fish tail. Charybdis ("sucker down"), daughter of the sea god Poseidon and Earth goddess Gaia, swallows huge amounts of water three times a day and then spouts it back out again, forming an enormous whirlpool. Water spirals as it drains from our sinks. The oceans are filled with all manner of spiral-shaped mollusks, such as the chambered nautilus and the conch shell. When air and weather come together in a certain way, the spiraling currents of the oceans generate powerful hurricanes. Humans even name these storms. Spiraling tornadoes spin over Earth's surface. On land we find spiral patterns in the ram's horn, the snail shell, and the tiniest sunflower seeds. The spirals of the spider's web connect earth and air, and a falling feather describes a spiral path.

Sufi whirling dervishes achieved a god ecstasy, and every child knows the dizzy feeling that comes from spinning in the grass. Just as there's more than one kind of spiral in Nature, there's more than one type of magical spiral dance. Some spirals are used as a meeting and greeting dance at the beginning of a Witchen circle. The people join hands in a circle and at a command they drop hands and turn facing outward, then rejoin their hands. The leader then makes a sharp turn inward and retraces the steps of the circle. In doing this, the leader first faces the person whose hand she's holding, and then every person in the line in turn. This dance allows every person to greet every other person with a smile of recognition and, in earlier times, a kiss of greeting. When they've gone completely around once, they are again facing inward, with hands joined, ready to begin their rite.

The magical spiral dance used in my NeoPagan practice, rather than serving as a meeting dance, is done at the culmination of a ritual. Celebrants join hand to hand in a single line, led by a priestess or priest. Starting with a single large circle, she leads the dance to the left, or widdershins (counterclockwise), round and round into a tight coil. When she reaches the center, she turns to her right and moves the line deosil (sunwise), snaking between the line of people who are still coiling to the center. As she does this, each person confronts the holiness in each other dancer. The dancers chant as they dance and drummers in the center of the circle mark the rhythm. The leader continues outward, then snakes back inward again, many times, depending on the size of the space, the number of people, the energy of the group (whether people seem to be losing stamina or not), and the purpose of the dance. At the end, the dancers are wound into a tight coil, their voices rise with the energy, then they reach up their hands to direct the energy to its intended use in empowering the working. We do this sacred dance at Samhain, our holiday in honor of our Beloved Dead. This is the dance of renewal, of life and death and back to life again. With a large crowd of one thousand or more people, two priests or priestesses lead two lines of dancers in the double helix formation of the DNA molecule. The magic of a spiral dance leaves the dancers with a powerful sense of connectedness—to each other, the world, and all the worlds.

See **The *Odyssey*.**

25

Trick or Treating

Trick or treating, a familiar American Halloween custom, probably has its origins in the British Isles during the medieval period from the end of the fifth to early sixth century C.E. Several holidays are associated with masking, costumes, and grotesques, including All Souls' Day and midwinter celebrations. On All Souls' Night, children would go from house to house begging Soul Cakes, pastries given to the children in return for their prayers for the dead. During this time of year, as in early April Fool's Day celebrations acknowledging the Lord of Misrule, the master of revels who turned ordinary rules on their head for his appointed time, people would cross-dress so that spirits bent on mischief would not recognize or harm them. Children were dressed in rags and their faces blackened with charcoal and ash or painted so that the faeries would not steal them and leave changelings in their place.

At Yule, the Wren Boys would roam the countryside, faces masked or painted, dressed in straw in barely human shapes, bearing the tiny body of a dead wren. The Wren Boys would sing hymns to the wren as the King of Birds. In one Welsh folktale, the wren earned this title by flying higher than even the eagle—by hiding on the eagle's back until it had reached the zenith of its power, then leaping from its hiding place to fly up above the eagle's head.

Samhain, the New Year in Ireland, begins with mischief. In days past, mischief makers unlatched farmers' gates, moved people's horses to different fields, and performed other acts of minor, relatively harmless mayhem. In Dublin, during the nineteenth and early twentieth centuries, children went from house to house begging for apples and nuts for their parties to celebrate Hallows. In County Waterford, Samhain was sometimes called *oidhche na h-aimléise*—the night of mischief. Boys and young men went about the district, blowing on horns, and asking for milk, bread, and butter at each house, dashing to see who could reach the door latch first, and playing tricks on people along the way.

Giving in to these demands, backed by the threat of tricks, echoes the laws and customs regarding hospitality in Celtic countries. It was considered a terrible thing to be stingy, and so when a stranger came to the door to ask for food, or a bed for the night, such things were not refused. In many of the old tales, those strangers might show themselves to be gods or spirits, and hospitality would be rewarded with prosperity, while stinginess would be punished with curses and misfortune.

In England, in early November, children celebrate Guy Fawkes' Day by dressing in rags and costumes as well, begging money for fireworks to burn the Guy (an effigy of a man who led an uprising against James I in 1605). This festival is very close to the Samhain holiday, and the two celebrations became entwined as the years passed. When Halloween came to North America, the customs of All Hallows followed the immigrants. Girls stayed inside and played divination games while young boys were out playing pranks, masked and costumed. The older folk would say that such mischief had been done by the spirits. It is easy to connect the treats given to the costumed boys with offerings to the spirits and the ancestors given in previous centuries, when Samhain was first celebrated to honor our Beloved Dead.

26

Yggdrassil

Some scholars say that the idea of Yggdrasil as world tree may have come from the ancients' observation of the polar star, about which the entire cosmos appears to revolve. The giant ash, growing from the center of the earth with roots that descend into the depths of the Underworld, is said to be the central axis around which the entire universe is arranged. The tree is so tall, in fact, that the top branches brush against the very vault of heaven. As the *Eddas*, which are the chief source documents for the Northern European mythology, say, "Of all the trees, the greatest and best is Yggdrasil." According to Scandinavian legend, ash in itself is a magical species of tree. The *Eddas* tell us that Ask, the first human male, was created from an ash tree and brought to life by the breath of the gods.

Yggdrasil itself is a busy place. Nidhogg, a dragon or giant serpent, gnaws constantly at one of Yggdrasil's roots, trying to destroy this tree that represents the life force of the cosmos. An eagle roosts in Yggdrasil's crown. A gossipy squirrel named Ratatosk continually scampers up and down the tree, carrying news back and forth between the eagle and the dragon. The world's birds use the twigs of Yggdrasil to build their nests. Deer graze in Yggdrasil's branches, constantly stripping and eating the leaves. And every day the Norse gods and goddesses descend the rainbow bridge from Asgard to hold council beneath Yggdrasil's far-reaching branches.

Yggdrasil has three main roots, all of which lead to magical wells or springs. At one root is the Well of Wyrd tended by the three Norns—the sisters Urd, Verdandi, and Skuld—whose continuous cycle of spinning, weaving, and raveling the tapestry of life determines the course of humanity. Two swans feed at this well also. It was believed, in fact, that the water here was so holy that it continually renewed Yggdrasil, no matter how much the roots were gnawed or the leaves devoured by the deer. This well nourishes Yggdrasil so thoroughly, in fact, that dew that drips from its branches becomes the food of bees and is transformed into honey.

Odin, the one-eyed all-father, is closely associated with Yggdrasil.

He gladly sacrificed one of his eyes for the privilege of drinking from Myrmir's Well at the second of Yggdrasil's roots. In return he was given cosmic consciousness, as this well is the source of all knowledge and intelligence. Odin actually sacrificed himself to himself at Yggdrasil. He hung from Yggdrasil upside down, spear-pierced, for nine days and nights without closing his remaining eye. At the end of the nine days, his tongue began to sing with poetry and he was given the magical gift of the runes. Runes are, beyond divination tools, an alphabet that was actually used in the Viking era. Today, some Vikings' graffiti written in runes survive in such far-flung places as Venice and Istanbul or the World Wide Web. Nowadays, many Pagans—especially those from the Northern tradition who prefer to be known as "Heathens"—use the runes for magical workings.

See **The *Poetic Eddas* and the *Nibelungenlied,* The Fates, the Furies and the Norns, Spinning, Holy Waters.**

II

SOCIETY AND CULTURE

Culture is adaptive behavior developed to ensure our survival as human beings in different geographical and meteorological regions of the world. Culture is learned, culture is non-instinctive, and culture is cumulative. Culture changes and adapts. For example, contact among different cultures changes all those cultures. In today's multicultural environment, we celebrate holidays and customs with their roots in other times and places.

The invention of agriculture eight thousand to ten thousand years ago provided a larger and more dependable food supply, and resulted in the expansion of human population. More people meant more information and more ideas, causing cultural evolution to accelerate. As people settled down in permanent communities, new kinds of social and political systems arose. With the development of cities, however, contagious diseases spread more easily. And with all of these changes, including health issues, crowded spaces, and technological innovations, came cultural innovations.

Language, dance, and art are cultural constructs common, in their vast variety, to all of human society. Drumming and music differ from one society to another, yet in many ways they speak a universal tongue that is able to cross cultural boundaries and transcend spoken language.

You may be intimately familiar with many entries in this section.

27

Agriculture

Who can say who were the first human beings to observe and remember the seasons when different plants flowered and seeded? Who noticed that certain soil, water, and light conditions caused particular plants to flourish? We do know that after the last Ice Age—between eight thousand and eleven thousand years ago—when melting glaciers exposed more land mass for humans to explore, and possibly to habitat, people invented what is now known as agriculture.

People learned about seeds, bulbs, nuts, and cuttings. They dug holes, planted seeds, and watered those seeds. Before the invention of mining and metallurgy, and hence the plow, people used hand tools to dig the holes for planting. They may have sown just before the rains in order to maximize the likelihood that their crops would get enough water to thrive. Later, they invented irrigation.

Evidence of early agriculture exists in the Fertile Crescent of the Tigris and Euphrates Rivers in what is present-day Iraq. Myth and literature tell us that the goddess Inanna caused these waters to rise and refresh the cultivated fields in spring. History reveals that the ancient Egyptian farmers relied on the annual flooding of the Nile for both water and renewal of the fertility of the land.

Around 8000 B.C.E. barley and emmer wheat began being cultivated in Mesopotamia, and around 6000 B.C.E. maize and beans were grown in America. These earlier farmers learned when to harvest and how to store foodstuffs so they would remain fresh enough to eat later in the season when food was less plentiful. Their agricultural efforts were greatly enhanced by the other Pagan inventions of irrigation to lift, move, and store water; draft animals and metal to allow for plowing in furrows; basketry to aid in the harvest; pottery for storage; and ovens for cooking.

In addition to providing an abundant, reliable food source, agriculture gave us gardens, where we often retire to find peace, beauty, and tranquility. In gardens we dine, enjoy entertainment, and perform religious rites such as marriages. The most celebrated ancient garden was the Hanging Gardens of Babylon, rising green and lush from the flat dry plain of Mesopotamia.

Our Pagan ancestors in many places throughout the world knew about irrigation, soil depletion, and symbiotic (mutually beneficial) crop mixtures. This knowledge allowed them to create sustainable agroecosystems without capital. They used locally available resources and human and animal energy.

In our present global circumstances we can look to the wisdom of our Pagan ancestors about growing food crops and other agricultural products in our efforts to feed our vastly more populous planet. We can apply many of these inherited ecological principles in the design of improved food production systems.

See **Baking, Brewing, Linen, The Descent of Inanna.**

28

Art

Deep in remote passages and chambers in the Earth we've found evidence of the art of our ancestors. In the Paleolithic (Old Stone Age), about 15,000 B.C.E., people painted the walls of caves near Lascaux in what is now France with images of horses, bison, mammoth, ibex (a wild mountain goat), aurochs (a long-horned wild ox, ancestor of modern domestic cattle, now extinct), reindeer, and panthers—all in action. These paintings could only have been done by lamplight, probably fueled with animal fat and wicked with moss. Their remoteness suggests these painted chambers had a ceremonial use.

Prehistoric cave paintings have also been discovered on the Iberian Peninsula in Spain and Portugal, in various places in France, in the

Italian Alps. These subterranean galleries not only provide evidence of how our forebearers lived, but also demonstrate how much they valued artistic expression. Because these mysterious paintings were done in deep, inaccessible places, because they depict life and death, hunting and killing for food so the people could survive, and because some of the places where they are found took many hours to reach, I believe that these images had religious significance to the people who created them.

Cave paintings in Chauvet, France, the majority of which depict megafauna such as lions, mammoths, and rhinoceroses, are dated at 32,000 B.C.E. Humans occupied the Altamira caves in Spain at two different times: eighteen thousand years ago and then again about fourteen thousand years ago. Beyond their living quarters, deeper in the caves, they engraved and painted red bison, elk, and several hands.

Ancient peoples left visual expressions on Earth's surface as well. Throughout Europe, Scandinavia, and North and Central America we find ancient pictographs, or painted images, and petroglyphs, which are carved, chiseled, or otherwise inscribed in rock. The Valmonica rock art in the Italian Alps depicts deer, dogs, horses, humans, daggers, parallel lines, and concentric circles.

In the far north of Norway, in Alta, people carved rock with images only visible around sunset when the angle of sunlight is low. Carved in four distinct phases, beginning as early as six thousand years ago and most recently five hundred years B.C.E., they depict people, reindeer, bear, elk, fish, birds, boats, and weapons. Some appear to be hunting scenes. Others show musicians playing instruments, one of which is a *runebommen*, the shamanic drum still used today in rituals by the Saami people of Norway, Finland, Sweden, and Russia.

Near Tulelake, California, between 500 and 1600 C.E., Modocs painted wavy lines, zigzags, rain symbols, dots, cross hatching, human figures, and star or wheel images on the high desert rocks. The creation of these drawings preceded contact with Europeans.

In digs of what are present-day France, Switzerland, and Germany archaeologists find exquisite metalwork done in the Iron Age (first millennium B.C.E.). Many of the "Celtic" spiral designs so popular now—in artwork, textile prints, jewelry, graphic arts, and tattoos—are not only inspired by these ancient designs, but also actually are often the same ones. What is it about these graceful swirls that so appeals to our artistic sensibilities? Is it their fluidity and the organic feel they have that's so different from the measured, the angular, the lined?

See **Basketry, Drums and Drumming, Pottery, Prehistoric "Venus" Figurines.**

29

Basketry

The use of plants to create vessels is a prehistoric art, predating even pottery. In fact, some very early examples of coil-formed pots show the exterior impressions of the baskets in which they were formed. Basketry in one form or another is a universal art form, having found its way to all four corners of Earth.

To create them, local materials were collected during the proper season for optimal quality and with due reverence, often with offerings made to the spirits of the plants that were being taken. Slim, straight branches, especially of certain species of willow, are extremely flexible, versatile, and easy to work with. These branches, or *withes*, are generally stripped of their bark and are often split into smaller strips for finer weaving. Thin hardwood strips, called *splints*, are also used in many places. Locally available tree and water-plant roots, grasses, stringy bark, colorful plant parts, seaweed, cornhusks, and many more materials have been used to create baskets by indigenous people around the world.

Whether one needed a baby carrier, a cooking pot, a winnowing tray, or a drinking cup, baskets were created for these uses and many more. Perhaps some of the most famous baskets were (and are) those created by the Native Americans of central California and western Nevada, which are so tightly woven that they can hold water and which, by putting hot rocks inside, can be used to cook large batches of acorn soup.

Some California Indian tribes completely covered their gift and ceremonial baskets with colorful bird feathers; then, after trade began with Europeans, with thousands of tiny glass beads. Additionally, baskets often had special places in ceremonies and rituals occasionally containing secret shaman's tools, ritual theater props, live animals, and other ceremonial items that needed to be concealed or contained in a special manner.

Baskets are part of ancient legends and lore as well as daily culture. They can also depict legends in their design—the Tohono O'odham and Pima Indians of the American Southwest sometimes weave baskets featuring a labyrinth with a small man inside to represent Iitoi, a restless ancestor spirit.

Taboos regarding baskets vary from culture to culture. Some people used human figures as design elements; others saw any representation of the human form as taboo. For example, among the Pomo and other California Indian tribes, a woman's baskets were burned when she died out of respect for their maker, weavers could not use their skills during menstruation, and they were not allowed to directly copy another woman's designs, some of which had spiritual significance. Lest others steal some of their power, weavers there would not even share the basin their materials were soaked in.

As far as we can determine, women were the primary basket makers and gatherers of weaving materials in ancient times. Picture a small group of women, perhaps a few with babies in cradle baskets nearby, singing together as they gather roots, stems, and branches from the Earth with respect, leaving offerings as they select just the right materials to make a fine basket. The circle is unbroken, if more solitary these days, every time a woman goes out to gather basket materials from the heart of the land.

See **Enheduanna.**

30

Coinage and Currency

Currency exchange began with the development of agriculture and the domestication of cattle around 9000–6000 B.C.E. Cattle was one of the first and most widespread forms of currency. Other animals frequently used for barter were pigs, goats, sheep, horses, and camels. People bartered with other goods such as hides and furs, flints, and other hard stones suitable for weapons, and they later bartered with ores and metals, as well as consumable goods like grain, fish, game, and dairy. Egypt and China were relatively advanced civilizations with administrative and tax systems. These lands assigned standard values to primary products like rice, tea, almonds, pepper, grain, olives, and figs.

With the inventions of smithcraft, smelting (heating rock to extract metal ores), and mining, as well as the crafting of metal objects, tools, weapons, and jewelry, ore and metal became valuable currency. Precious and semiprecious stones were additional goods that served well as currency; they were easily portable and had a high value.

In 1200 B.C.E., the Chinese employed little white or yellow porcelain-like shells called "cowries" as currency. Arab traders dispersed this practice through India, the Near East, and as far as Africa, where they remained in use up until the middle of the twentieth century C.E.

Salt was an essential commodity throughout the ancient world. The salt roads, caravan routes upon which traders carried salt for trading, extended from the Baltic to Italy, from the Himalayas to India, from the Sahara to Egypt. Salt was used for currency and soldiers were paid with salt, which is where the word "salary" originates.

Crude coins, as well as permanent retail shops where they were used, were produced in Lydia, Asia Minor, around 687 B.C.E. About forty-five years later the Lydians began making coins of electrum, a naturally occurring amalgam of gold and silver. At about the same time, coinage came into use in India and China.

The most common form of ancient coin was hammered. A blank piece of metal of the correct weight was placed between two dies, then hammered. The hammering made the stamp imprint on the metal, which produced the proper image on both sides. Early coins were then subject to shaving, wherein the edge was removed, thus diminishing the weight of the coin and accumulating metal for the person who shaved the coins—called a pilferer. An alternative method of coin making was done by casting coins in molds. Individual coins made this way were called cash, from which we get our modern English word.

Between 595 and 570 B.C.E., the Greek cities of Aegina, Athens, and

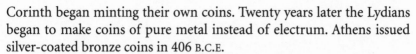

Corinth began minting their own coins. Twenty years later the Lydians began to make coins of pure metal instead of electrum. Athens issued silver-coated bronze coins in 406 B.C.E.

The Romans adopted coinage much later than did most of the Mediterranean populations of the day. They issued silver coins beginning in 269 B.C.E. The Roman Moneta, goddess of warning, caused geese to cackle to alert the Romans of a pending Gaulish invasion. The grateful Romans built her a shrine. The words "money" and "mint" are derived from her name. By 200 B.C.E., after the second Punic War between Rome and Carthage, the barren Island of Delos, with its temple of Apollo and fine harbor, became the financial capital of its day.

When Julius Caesar raided Gaul and Britain, he found evidence that the Celtic tribes minted coins of gold, silver, bronze, and a copper-tin alloy called *potin*. His nephew, Augustus, instituted monetary reforms that included the issuance of gold, silver, brass, and copper coins, as well as three new taxes: a general sales tax, a land tax, and a flat-rate poll tax.

So it's Pagans we can blame for money. We still see images of Roman deities on our coins today: "Mercury"dimes bear the image of the goddess Nike, or winged victory.

See **Law, Smithcraft, Mercury/Hermes, Nike.**

31

Democracy

The ancient Pagan Athenians are to be thanked for democracy. From the Greek *demos*, meaning "the people," and *kratein*, meaning "to rule," this method of government was developed and practiced there from the early sixth to mid-fifth centuries B.C.E. At its height in the fifth century, the population of Athens was about 300,000 people, quite a large city.

Athenian democracy was a direct, or pure, democracy. This means that all citizens voted on all civic and governmental matters in person at a physical gathering in a public space. Nearly all citizens participated in Athenian democracy, a much higher proportion of eligible participants than that of any contemporary state or form of democracy. However, only citizens were eligible to engage in this process. If a citizen was serving in the military or traveling when decisions were being made, he could not participate.

Citizenship in Athens was restricted to males and citizens had to be born so. Only rarely could they gain admittance through an elaborate procedure that could be vetoed by any citizen. No *metis* (resident

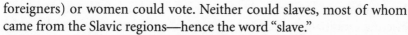

foreigners) or women could vote. Neither could slaves, most of whom came from the Slavic regions—hence the word "slave."

As in Athens, most democracies have been limited to an elite class of people, usually only propertied males. Fortunately, in the United States today, since the Civil Rights Act of 1965, citizens enjoy universal suffrage. The only citizens barred from voting are those who have been convicted of a felony.

Papyrus, vellum, and parchment were expensive in sixth-century B.C.E. Athens, so fragments of pottery (*ostracon*) were used for casual note taking and balloting. For unknown reasons, once a year votes were taken on which a single citizen could be ostracized. This was the only vote done by ballots, made by scratching a name on an ostracon. The assembly needed to have six thousand ballots cast in order to ostracize one citizen for a period of ten years. Although death was the penalty should the banished person return, he retained his property and could appoint an agent to deal with his affairs and forward any revenues. Special laws were enacted enabling an ostracized person to be recalled in special circumstances.

In the Athenian system of democracy, leaders were chosen at random to fill official administrative positions by a lottery system called "sortition." The only way sortition exists today is in the way a court chooses a jury. A man could serve in a particular office only once in his life; thereafter, he was exempted from serving in that capacity.

The only elected position was that of *strategos*, the chief of military officials but not exactly a general in that strategos commanded both land and sea forces. Not only was this a dangerous position to hold, but also the candidate needed to have wealth and popularity in order to be elected. The office of strategos was a paid position.

Today, other forms of democracy exist besides the direct democracy practiced in ancient Athens. The most familiar is representative democracy, by which voters choose delegates to represent their interests in lawmaking. In delegative democracy, delegates can be recalled by their constituents if the constituents don't think the delegate is representing their interests. Delegates serve for prescribed terms in representative democracy.

See **Papyrus, Parchment/Vellum, and Paper.**

32

Domestication of Animals

It's difficult to determine with any certainty when and where animals were first domesticated and began to live with human beings and depend on them for food and protection. Around 10,000 B.C.E., however, dogs became domesticated in Mesopotamia from their ancestors, the jackals. Others were tamed from wolves. The domestication of dogs enhanced people's ability to hunt: their acute sense of smell aided in tracking prey, and the running and barking helped early hunters to locate hiding prey and approach them for the kill.

At about the time when people were learning to cultivate plants (eight to eleven thousand years ago), and thus were able to acquire enough food in storage to allow them to begin settling into more permanent villages and even cities, the domesticated dog advanced the cultivation of herd animals. Sheep and goats are fairly small and easier to herd than larger animals like cattle. About 7000 B.C.E. goats, descended from the Persian wild goat, were domesticated in Crete. Around the same time, the wild urial from southwest Asia became the domestic sheep. A group of people with a herd of animals had a reliable source of protein for their diets, although they did have to keep on the move in order to provide their herds with good grazing.

Horses descend from the smaller, rougher wild Asiatic horse in the steppes of northern Asia. We don't know how early horses were domesticated in Asia, but evidence suggests that Europeans used domestic horses around 4000–3500 B.C.E. Human beings walk at about three miles per hour, horses at about twenty-five miles per hour. Thus it's easy to see how horses enabled people to travel vast expanses of land. This development not only expanded their hunting grounds, but also enabled people to herd larger animals such as cattle, descended from the now-extinct aurochs. Horses served as draft animals, as did cattle and oxen. Other species domesticated to serve as pack animals are the llama in the Andes Mountains of South America, the camel in Africa and Asia, the yak in Tibet, the alpaca, and the wild ass. The Saami people, derogatively called but more commonly known as Laplanders, of what is now northern Scandinavia, farmed reindeer as their primary food source.

As human beings began to live in more-or-less permanent settlements, they were able to domesticate other smaller animal flocks unsuited for herding. Among these were the chicken—from the red jungle fowl of India—followed by turkeys, ducks, and geese, and the pig—from the wild boar found in the forests of Europe. The rabbit was cultivated for food and fur; the goldfish for food; and the pigeon, from the rock dove of Europe, for food and communication. And, sweetest of all, bees were cultivated to provide honey.

The cat seems to have been domesticated by early Egyptians from the African wildcat primarily for its beauty alone; only later did the cat develop into a rat catcher. The oft-despised feline has saved closed cities from complete decimation by the plague due to its hunting and killing of the rodents, the vectors of the disease.

Domestic animals provide not only meat, but also hides and wool for clothing and tools; bone, antler, and horn for tools; bladders for carrying water and wine; eggs; dairy; drayage and transportation; honey; and currency (wealth was often determined by the size of a people's herds). Some, like the horse and dog, provide entertainment (racing) and, along with the cat, some birds, and fishes, companionship. And let us not forget the wonderful working dogs that assist the blind and people with other handicaps to live full, productive, self-determined lives.

The elephant was tamed in India and Southeast Asia for its ability to move trees and heavy objects as well as for transportation. (The elephant may not be entirely domesticated, because most elephants could survive in the wild if they were released among their kind.) Animals that have been fully domesticated need human care to live. Such animals as the chicken must live under human care, but other animals such as the pig, cat, and horse can survive as feral animals.

Since all of these cultural developments preceded the emergence of the Abrahamic religions of Judaism, Christianity, and Islam, we can be certain that their inventors were of a paleo-Pagan religious perspective.

33

Drums and Drumming

Ceremonial frame drumming is portrayed in ancient Mesopotamian art of three to four thousand years ago, Greek vases show women drumming and dancing, and Roman murals depict musicians and dancers using frame drums. Drums go back to the beginning of the human race, however, probably originating in Africa, where drummers of "talking drums" learned to imitate the pitch patterns of language in order to communicate over long distances. Drumming has accompanied storytelling, singing, and dancing everywhere. People have also produced rhythmic sounds by hand-clapping, body-slapping, and slapping or hitting hollow logs. Gourds or leather bags filled with seeds or pebbles make fine rattles. The *shekere* is a gourd with beads netted around the outside to make the sound. The Ojibway people of central North America danced with a rattle made of a tortoise shell, neck, head, and belly. The neck and head were used as grips and the shell and belly was filled with the beaks of a hundred birds which, when the rattle was shaken, magi-

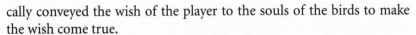

cally conveyed the wish of the player to the souls of the birds to make the wish come true.

Drums are used to stimulate healing, to foster and sustain connection with the spirit world, and to convey coded instructions to soldiers. Specific drums and rhythms are used for specific purposes and specific dances. Nearly every culture worldwide uses the instrument in the important rites of passage of birth, puberty, marriage, ascension to power, death, and burial. African drums were used to protect tribal royalty and are housed in a sacred dwelling.

Frame drums—shallow circular wooden frames with skins stretched over one side—were played in ancient Egypt, one such being the North African *tar*. The goblet-shaped *dumbek*, made of clay, wood, or metal, is traditionally played under the arm throughout the Middle East and North Africa.

Frame drums may be round, square, or triangular in shape and range in size from six to thirty inches in diameter. Frame drums are the sacred instrument of the tribal shamans (travelers between the worlds of people and spirits) of Siberia and North American Native tribal shamans. They are also found in the Basque country, Finland, China, Russia, Mongolia, Algeria, and Morocco. NeoPagans are reviving the use of the frame drum, affirming and reconnecting us with our foremothers.

The tambourine is a portable single-headed frame drum with or without jingling metal disks in the frame. Illustrations of ancient dancing women show them playing tambourines. The *riq* or *duff* are Middle

Eastern frame drums with loud jingles, the tambourine-like instrument of Central Asia is called the *gaval*, the lively *pandiero* is played in Brazil, and the *tamburello* is used in southern Italy for healing rituals. The Spanish, Galician, and Portuguese play a square drum with metal jingles also called a *pandeiro* (masculine) or *pandeira* (feminine). The frame drum known as the *bendir* is played in Morocco, Persia, and other Islamic countries.

Perhaps the most popular frame drum in the West today is the Irish *bodhran*, probably introduced to the isle by Arabic traders or via the Roman Empire. Designs on the frame and head of the bodhran and other drums carry magical meanings: the crosspiece on the back corresponds to the Elements of Life—Air, Fire, Water, and Earth—with Spirit at the central meeting point and surrounding the whole. Sacred animals and bird totems or symbols of gods and spirits may be painted or stained on the skin, and designs may be painted or carved into the wooden rim.

The little handheld clapper instruments called castanets have been around for more than two thousand years. They are mentioned in Greco-Roman literature, where they are called *krotalon* or *krembalon*, meaning "a dancer's instrument." Wooden castanets are played in both of the dancer's hands, just as are the brass finger cymbals of belly dancers.

Giant kettle drums date from 4000 B.C.E. Turkey. The Persians of the Achaemenid period (533–330 B.C.E.) used the *kus* and the *karnay*, both types of kettle drum, in battle. The hemispheric *kuses* were so large they were carried on horse-, camel-, or elephant-back. When the drum was beaten with a leather-and-wood drumstick, the sound carried for miles. They are the forerunner of the modern orchestral *timpani.*

The *taiko,* or "giant drum," of Japan was used in religious festivals and ceremonies in temples and shrines going back at least two thousand years. Taiko drums were paraded through the streets calling people to join the festival. They may be as large as six feet in diameter, with cow skins on both ends, producing a thunderous sound to invoke the rain gods at rice-planting ceremonies. They were also used in the battlefields to issue commands, coordinate movements, and intimidate the enemy. But perhaps the most unusual use of taiko drums is to control insect infestations.

In Vedic India of the first few millennia B.C.E., music and rhythm were used in religious rites, where they helped the people approach their gods with awe, respect, and devotion, just as they still do. The two drums comprising the *tabla* are the best known.

The large and powerful West African *djembe* is played not only in Africa, but at almost every NeoPagan festival in North America.

See **Lipushau.**

34

Encyclopedia

In the fourth century B.C.E., the grand Library of Alexandria, located at the crossroads of the three continents of Europe, Asia, and Africa, housed an estimated 700,000 volumes of writings in many languages and forms. Some were written on papyri, made of reed-like plant material, or on vellum, a very fine grade of parchment, made of animal skin. A scholar named Callimachus was commissioned to create a catalog of these works. The *Pinakes,* as it was called, was a critical appraisal of the collection, a bibliographical survey of the writings "in every field of learning." This was a tremendous undertaking, requiring encyclopedic knowledge and erudition. Surviving fragments of the Pinakes attest to divisions of "rhetoric, law, epic, tragedy, comedy, lyric poetry, history, medicine, mathematics, natural science, and miscellanea." Each division contained an alphabetical list of individual authors, with a critical account of his or her writings. In addition, each entry included the book's place of origin, length of text (number of lines), and whether the manuscript was mixed (i.e., containing more than one work) or un-mixed (i.e., containing only a single work).

Scholars from many parts of the world came to the library and availed themselves of this indispensable resource. The Pinakes served as a model for future works of its kind. It was the first encyclopedia.

See **Libraries and Books, Papyrus, Parchment/Vellum, and Paper.**

35

Law

The Codex Hammurabi is the oldest intact written law code known, preceded only by the Code of Lipit-Ishtar (circa 1868 B.C.E.) and of which only fragments exist today.

Hammurabi came from a Semitic people called Amorites who settled in Mesopotamia around 2000 B.C.E. Hammurabi was Babylon's priest-king, who, in 1792 B.C.E., unified Mesopotamia, creating an empire he ruled for forty-three years. The cities of Babylon and Ur each had populations upward of 200,000 people, with carefully laid-out streets, canals, and irrigation.

Their chief god was Marduk, who eventually was addressed as Bel, meaning "lord." The sun god, Shamash, was patron of law and justice. As divine ruler and priest of Shamash, Hammurabi caused a set of 282 laws to be written covering economics, family, crime, and civil matters. An example of his code calls for severe retributions, such as an eye for an eye and a tooth for a tooth; it preceded the more merciful Talmud by 2,500 years.

The laws are written in the Akkadian language in sixteen columns of cuneiform-wedged script on a black diorite stone stele (an upright stone pillar) eight feet tall. The upper front of the stele shows Hammurabi standing before Shamash. The king's right hand is raised in prayer, as Shamash is handing him the rod of kingship and the ring of divine justice. Rays signifying holiness, divinity, and power emanate from Hammurabi's head. The text begins and ends with addresses to the gods. In a world without books and paper, literate people were able to read the laws on the steles that were placed in public temples for that purpose. All were expected to obey the laws.

At a much later date, in a place distant from the Fertile Crescent, the people of Ireland developed a complex system of law known as the Brehon Laws. The interpretation and application of the law was conducted by a highly trained, influential class of people called Brehons, which means judges.

There are two large and important tracts of these laws, each comprising five to six volumes, and written on vellum. Compiled by nine people over a three-year period beginning in 438 C.E., the code articulated civil, military, and criminal law, and it enumerated the rights and privileges of all classes of ancient Irish society. The tract set forth detailed laws relating to land and property. Unlike real estate today, much of the land was held in common rather than being the property of a single family, clan, or tribe, and there were no fences at all. Non-arable land—mountain, forest, bog—was free to be used by all free people for grazing, procuring fuel, and hunting.

Brehons presided at trials outdoors. Plaintiffs and defendants were represented by counsel and rules of evidence were applied. The most highly regarded Brehons delivered their judgments in the forms of sententious maxims, or apt illustrations. The best of these judgments became proverbs. In contrast to the harsh code of Hammurabi, the Brehon Laws did not include capital punishment. The most severe was banishment. The Brehon Laws were well suited to the society out of which they arose, so much so that English settlers in Ireland were forbidden to use the Brehon Laws on penalty of treason.

The laws used to govern today are much changed from those of the past, but the codifying of standards of civilized conduct in a diverse social, economic, political, and economic world is another gift from our Pagan ancestors.

36

Libraries and Books

Writing and books arose from within ancient Pagan cultures. The concept of assembling the accumulated written knowledge and thought into a single repository, or several repositories, is Pagan too.

Around 295 B.C.E., one of Alexander the Great's generals became the pharaoh Ptolemy I Soter. To enhance his leader's international stature, Ptolemy set about making Alexandria a rival of Athens as a center of culture and learning. Here he built his renowned Library of Alexandria. Prior to that time, temples and museums housed religious and official texts, while a few wealthy private individuals maintained collections of Greek manuscripts. Other ancient civilizations in Egypt, Mesopotamia, Syria, Asia Minor, and Greece had established libraries of a regional nature, in an effort to conserve their respective national traditions and heritage. Ptolemy's project was the first effort to amass a complete collection of the known world.

These works were written on papyri or vellum scrolls and stored in pigeonholes or racks. The best were wrapped in linen or leather jackets. The collection grew to an estimated 700,000 volumes, and it included most Greek literature of the time, including the works of Aristotle and Plato; the original manuscripts of Sophocles, Aeschylus, and Euripides; and all of the Egyptian records; as well as books on the Oriental religions of Zoroastrianism and Buddhist writings on astronomy, mathematics, medicine, geography, and mechanics.

Ptolemy I instructed that the works of other cultures be translated into Greek. The first translation was of the Pentateuch of the Old Testament, done by seventy-two rabbis hired and housed by Ptolemy. In addition, the library permanently housed an estimated thirty to fifty scholars and employed scribes.

Amazing intellectual advancements took place at the Library of Alexandria: It was where Euclid developed his theories of geometry. The first studies of conic sections (ellipse, parabola, and hyperbola), spherical triangles, prime numbers, formulae for measuring three-dimensional figures, and other advanced mathematical theories were done at the library. The astronomer Eratosthenes calculated Earth's diameter to within 0.5 percent of what we now know it to be. He believed that Earth is round; and his coworker, Aristarchus of Samos, hypothesized that Earth and the planets revolve around the sun fifteen centuries before Copernicus and Galileo were born. The system of latitude and longitude were invented; the constellations were mapped. These data and theories contributed to the science of navigation and the calculations of accurate calendars to estimate annual flooding and the proper timing of the sowing and reaping of crops. At Alexandria, Herophilus discovered that the brain rather than the heart was the seat of thought. The library also saw the development of optics and hydraulics. From approximately the third century B.C.E. to the fourth century C.E., the library dominated the ancient world of learning.

Julius Caesar laid seige to Alexandria in 48 B.C.E. and set fire to the city. The library and its vast storehouse of learning was destroyed, but there is evidence emerging today that many of the library's scholars sought refuge in Turkey at the city of Harran.

A brand new library called Bibliotheca Alexandrina, established by the Egyptian government, in cooperation with UNESCO, opened in 2002. Countries around the world funded this project. In the international spirit fostered at the original Library of Alexandria, Italians and Egyptians are working together to preserve rare old manuscripts, the French are organizing a science museum, Americans are helping with computer systems, and dozens of countries are sending books.

Minnesota Witch Steven Posch says, "Christians, Jews, and Muslims are known as the People of the Book. Pagans, however, have always realized that one book is never enough. Pagans are not the people of the book; Pagans are the people of the library." In the spirit of the great minds who lived and worked at the ancient Library of Alexandria, today we see a resurgence of this respect for the value of books and learning in the establishment of Pagan libraries. The New Alexandrian Library in Delaware is under way, and the New Alexandria Library in Minneapolis already exists as a private library open to all sincere researchers. In addition to our own libraries, public, college, and university libraries continue to expand their collections of writings on things Pagan.

See **Hypatia, Papyrus, Parchment/Vellum, and Paper, Encyclopedia, Writing.**

37

Logic

Logic is a system of reasoning developed by our Pagan ancestors, the ancient Greeks. Logic is intended to guide people in determining which forms of inference are valid and which are not, and to articulate their reasoning.

Considered a branch of philosophy, logic was discussed, debated, and written about by the early Greek philosophers. Ideas such as reference, prediction, identity, truth, quantification, and existence are the province of philosophical logic. Philosophical logic deals with formal descriptions of natural language. Aristotle and his students held that the two most important principles of logic are the law of non-contradiction, stating that no proposition is both true and false, and the law of excluded middle, stating that a proposition must either be true or false. This kind of logic is called Aristotelian logic.

Traditionally, logic is divided into deductive reasoning and inductive reasoning. The process of deductive reasoning proceeds from the general to the specific. An example is: "All calico cats are female." "This cat has calico markings, therefore it is female." The process of inductive reasoning, first articulated by Aristotle, goes in the opposite direction, from the specific to the general. Inductive reasoning suggests probability, but is not necessarily as valid as deductive reasoning.

Formal logic, also known as symbolic logic, deals with the relationships between concepts that are rigorously defined. It provides a way to compose proofs of statements in precise, compact, unambiguous symbolic notation. Formal logic enables statement and argument to be codified into formulae. Besides being a branch of philosophy, logic is also considered to be a branch of mathematics, wherein the principles of formal logic are used to study mathematical reasoning.

Since computer science proceeds from mathematical logic, without the Pagan invention of logic, science would not have been able to progress to the age of the World Wide Web.

See **The Witches' Voice.**

38

May Day

The celebration of May Eve and May Day is ancient, widespread throughout the English-speaking world and beyond, and is very much alive today. Night-women in the service of Dame Holda, Germanic goddess associated with snow making and spinning, revel in the mountains of Germany on Walpurgisnacht, the night before May Day. Swedes dance wantonly around their holy places. The people of the British Isles erect giant, garlanded, ribbon-bedecked phallic Maypoles for the dance that weaves the ribbons and the spell for fertility of people, land, and livestock. In Ireland as far back as people can remember the fires are lit upon the hills to honor the solar god Bile and the return of longer days and growing crops. Cattle are driven between two fires for protection, before they're herded to summer pasture.

The ancient Romans celebrated the festival of Floralia for the first five days in May. They decorated the city with floral wreaths, wore flowers in their hair, played games, and danced. Celebrants left offerings of milk and honey at the temples of Flora, goddess of flowers, and her sisters Fauna, Maia, and Ops. They considered May to be an inauspicious month for marriage. When Maia is celebrated as Queen of Heaven, special cakes are baked in her honor and young unmarried girls are dressed in blue. There are many old May carols still sung today, such as "Sumer Is Icumen In" or "Hallantoe." In Padstow, England, the villagers perform a ribald dance with the "Padstow 'hoss" (horse). May wine is liberally consumed by all. May morn dew is said to have magical properties; it clears the complexion and cures minor ills. The goddess of the rainbow, the bridge connecting heaven and Earth, called Iris by the Greeks, is celebrated in May in both Greece and Japan.

All contracts are null and void at Beltaine on May 1. This includes wedding vows, so that if a woman should conceive during the May fertility revelry, her babe was said to be "Merry-begat," fathered by the god, and blessed with second sight.

Hierarchy was set aside, along with contracts, on May Day. Always associated with working people and tradesmen—those who plow the fields, tend the flocks, make the implements—May Day was one of the two most popular feast days for medieval craft guilds. It was, therefore, a natural choice for a day to celebrate workers' rights. In fact, at the first international gathering of the International Working Men's Association (IWW or Wobblies) in Paris in 1889, members declared May 1 an international working class holiday in commemoration of the Haymarket Martyrs, eight anarchist trade unionists who were victims of workers' rights clashes in Chicago three years earlier.

In 2001, Irish NeoPagans created Fire Eye Festival—to relight the

Beltaine fires—with people who came from around the world to attend, despite the foot and mouth disease scare.

Today Pagans and workers join together in celebrations. NeoPagans in "Paganistan" (Minneapolis-St.Paul) parade through the streets with colorful giant puppets and move on to a Maypole dance in the parks. In San Francisco, NeoPagan Witches honor the rich traditions of May Day; celebrate the vibrant political passions the day abets; and fill the streets with floats, music, dance, theater, and poetry—including giant puppets and the dancing of the Maypole. The celebration is called Reclaim May Day.

See **Cerne Abbas Giant, Thomas Morton.**

39

Olympic Games

Mythology suggests that the inception of the Olympic games came about when Hercules, the strongest of all men, challenged his four brothers to a race before the gods in the fields of Olympia. There is also evidence that games originated in the eleventh century B.C.E. in a small regional festival dedicated to Zeus, the patriarch of the Hellenic pantheon, but which had its origins among Mycenaeans who worshipped the goddess Rhea, sister of Zeus's father, Cronus.

Whatever its official origin, we do know that the first of the official games took place in Bronze Age Greece in 776 B.C.E., and consisted of only a six-hundred-foot-long foot race: in fact, for the first thirteen Olympiads (four-year cycles between games, as today), the foot race was the only competition. Outdoor foot races took place in a *stadion* big enough to hold twenty thousand spectators, and from which we get our word "stadium." Competitors came from throughout the city-states of the Greek world, from as far west as Iberia (Spain) and as far east as the Black Sea (Turkey); they came from Italy, Libya, Egypt, and the Ukraine. However, competition was limited exclusively to male citizens. As the games grew, competitions were added. In 708 B.C.E. longer races were introduced, as well as the pentathlon (the five field events of discus, javelin, long jump, wrestling, and foot race). About two hundred years after the Olympic games were instituted Roman men were allowed to compete, probably because they had captured Greece by then. In addition to athletics, entrants competed in writing, poetry, and history readings, and business transactions and treaties were made between leaders of the city-states.

Wrestling and boxing competitions took place in the *gymnasion* (place of naked people), appropriately in the nude. Competitions involving horses, such as chariot races, took place in the *hippodromos* ("horse racecourse"). A competitor was called an *athlete*, the contest was called *athlos,* and the prize was an *athlon.* The Olympic victors were crowned with olive as the Pythia, Apollo's oracle at Delphi, advised in 752 B.C.E. But there were other sites of athletic competition in ancient Greece where different wreaths were placed on the heads of the winners: laurel at Delphi, pine at Isthmia, and parsley at Nemea.

Victorious athletes also received substantial material prizes. Among them were such expensive bronze items as tripods, cauldrons, and shields, as well as woolen cloaks, olive oil, oxen, and women. Yes, women. In addition, when these victors returned to their home city-states, they were given large monetary gifts and were exempted from paying taxes. Proud Athenians gave their Olympic victors a free meal in the city hall every day, and later victorious athletes were granted pensions, which could be bought and sold.

Sculptors were commissioned to create idealized sculptures of winning athletes for display in the temple of Zeus. Only after an individual had won three competitions could his realistic likeness be displayed in the temple. Sometimes sculptures of winning athletes were also mounted in public places in their individual city-states.

During the golden age of Greece (477–431 B.C.E.), Olympia, where the games took place, was considered holy ground. It is here where Zeus lived; Mount Olympus is the highest mountain on mainland Greece and a rural sanctuary in the western Peloponnesos. Every four years (olympiad) heralds traveled the land proclaiming a month of truce while the Olympic games took place, to ensure the safety of athletes, visitors, spectators, and embassies. Violators of this truce were subject to substantial fines.

The ancient Olympic complex contained temples of and outdoor altars to both Zeus and Hera, baths, a swimming pool, treasury buildings, the stadion, and the hippodrome. Competitions for females were performed in honor of Hera. These competitions were organized and supervised by a committee of sixteen women from the nearby city-states. At each four-year cycle, a new *peplos* (loose outer robe worn by women in ancient Greece) was woven to present to Hera inside her temple. On this occasion, a foot race for girls took place in which only maidens could compete. They wore hair unbound down their backs and tunics that hung down almost to the knees, covering only their left shoulder and breast. Unmarried girls and women could watch the men's and boys' contests. Married women, however, were permitted neither to participate in the women's athletic competitions nor to enter the sanctuary of Zeus when boys and men were competing. Women who violated this prohibition were thrown off a cliff.

The original Olympic Games continued unbroken for twelve centuries. In 393 C.E. the Roman emperor Theodosius I banned the Olympic games and all Pagan festivals. There is evidence, however, that the games continued in spite of his edict. Finally, in 426 C.E., the army of Theodosius II, Theodosius I's successor, demolished the temples at Olympus. They continued to crumble from various earthquakes and floods over the next fifteen centuries, until they were rediscovered by German archaeologists in 1875.

French baron Pierre de Coubertin revived the Olympic Games in Athens in 1896. Today the international Olympic Games are held more frequently, and in both summer and winter. Women now compete on equal footing with men, and there are many more sports in the competition. The original athletes competed as individuals rather than as teams as is done today. In 1908, the modern Olympic flag of five linked rings, each with a primary color used in the flags of the competing nations, was introduced. The Olympic oath followed in 1920. The Olympic flame was inaugurated in 1932 in Los Angeles; the modern torch relays were added in 1936 in Berlin.

See **Delphic Oracle.**

40

Rhetoric

The word "rhetoric" comes from the Greek word *rhêtôr*, meaning "orator." The orator, or rhetorician, uses language to persuade people to his way of thinking. In modern times, the meaning of rhetoric has become trivialized to connote empty propaganda. In its beginning, however, rhetoric was one of the essential three *trivium*, or liberal arts, taught along with dialectic and grammar. First codified in a manual attributed to Corax and Tisias, both ancient Greek writers, rhetoric was popularized throughout the Mediterranean world during the fifth century B.C.E. by itinerant teachers known as sophists. The three best-known sophists were Protagoras, Gorgias, and Isocrates.

Gorgias, born in Sicily, traveled to Athens in 427 B.C.E. as head of an embassy of Sicilians seeking protection from Syracusan aggression. He remained in Athens, supporting himself by teaching rhetoric and practicing oratory. Gorgias aided in promoting the Attic dialect as the language of literary prose.

Plato, on the other hand, opposed rhetoric. He considered dialectic, the art of investigating truths through discussion, to be the more important process. Plato admitted to the possibility of the development of a true and noble rhetoric.

Plato's student, Aristotle, believed that the truths arrived at through dialectical process require rhetorical methods. Aristotle articulated three kinds of proof to be offered on behalf of an argument: *logos*, *pathos*, and *ethos*. Logos uses reasoned logic to construct an argument. Pathos (from which we get the words "pathetic," "sympathy," and "empathy") deals with emotional appeals, while ethos considers the character and credibility of the speaker to his audience. Today's applied social sciences are based on the art of persuasion, or rhetoric.

Two Roman rhetoricians, Cicero and Quintillian, saw the value of Aristotle's thinking, and extended it: Marcus Tullius Cicero was a Roman statesman and orator during the reign of Julius Caesar. He attained prominence as a consul and persuasive speaker. His prose style was considered the greatest in Latin. After the assassination of Julius Caesar, Cicero led the Senate in trying to restore the Republic peacefully. For this he was executed in 43 B.C.E.

Quintillian, born in Spain around 35 C.E., grew up in Rome where he learned rhetoric from his father. He headed a prominent school of oratory there for twenty years. When Quintillian retired from teaching in 88, he wrote his opus, *Institutio Oratoria*, about the training of orators. He proposed five canons, or general rules: (a)*inventio* (invention), the process of developing and refining an argument; (b) *dispositio* (disposition or arrangement) structures and organizes the speech for greatest effect; (c) *pronuntiatio* (language choice) involving the choice of words and grammar; (d) *elocutio* (delivery) considers how the speech will be spoken, its vocalization, intonation, and emphases; and finally (e) *memoria* (memory) involves committing the oration to memory.

Education spread widely throughout the Roman Empire during the hundred years between Cicero and Quintillian. In the far reaches of the empire in Gaul, Spain, and Africa, as well as in Rome, municipal funds endowed professorships and oratory contests drew enthusiastic crowds. The goal of education was to develop oratory skill, a primary necessity for anyone who would seek a public career. As it is today, the art of oration was important to success in the courts, where pleaders briefed sophisticated judges, juries, and audiences.

Politicians are well served by having good skills in oration, but in spite of that, masterful rhetoricians seem to be in short supply these days. Civilization would be well served were this ancient art to be revived.

41

Theater

The oldest form of theater of which we have record comes from Egypt around 2000 B.C.E., when an actor named I-kher-nefert (or Ikernofret) reenacted the passion of Osiris. Osiris was a legendary god-king who was murdered and dismembered by his brother Set. Osiris's wife, Isis, gathered his parts and restored Osiris to life, but without his lost penis. Repeated performances kept the suffering and triumph of the god in being restored to life vivid in the minds of the faithful who attended these plays annually at Abydos, Busiris, Heliopolis, and elsewhere in Egypt.

From about 1200 B.C.E., the cult of the god Dionysus arose, with worshippers participating in orgiastic ritual celebrations that included hysterical rampages by women called Maenads. These practices of uninhibited dancing and intoxication led to an altered state of consciousness called *ecstasis*, ultimately producing a cathartic release of emotions. A key part of the Dionysian rites was the *dithyramb*, an ode to the god sung by a chorus of fifty men dressed as satyrs (man-goat companions of the god), while worshippers chanted and danced around an image of Dionysus, to the sound of flute, lyres, and drums. The dithyramb eventually evolved into tragedy, which literally means "goat song."

The larger Greek city-states like Delphi built large amphitheaters for the performance of the dithyramb. Athens, between 600 and 200 B.C.E., flowered as the center of ancient Greek theater. There, drama competitions were instituted, financed by wealthy patrons, called *choregos*, who were exempted from paying taxes that year (an early form of tax shelter). Competitors were chosen by a government authority called an *archon*, and dramatic competitions grew so popular that attendance grew to thirty thousand.

The Theater of Dionysus in Athens seated seventeen thousand spectators in its *theatro*, the wooden spectator stands set up on the hillsides surrounding the performance area. The chorus sang from a platform in front of the main stage; this platform was called an *orchestra*. Plays were performed in the daytime, without scenery. Traditional tragedy began with a *prologue* describing the situation; followed by a *parados*, an ode sung by the chorus as it entered; five dramatic scenes; and an *exodus*, the climax or conclusion. Each dramatic scene was followed by an exchange of laments between the chorus and the protagonist.

The dramatist Thespis of Attica added an actor, called the *protagonist*, who interacted with the chorus. Today we call actors thespians in honor of Thespis. Thespis also invented the touring company, a troupe that used its cart for a stage. Aeschylus added a second actor, the *antagonist*, reduced the chorus from fifty to twelve, and added props and scenery. Around 486 B.C.E., the playwright Sophocles added a third actor to theater and emphasized human drama instead of actions between humans and gods. Euripides wrote more realistic plays concerned with the reality of war and criticism of religion, as well as peasants, slaves, women, and princes. Euripides also introduced the *deus ex machina* ("god from machine") to wrap up the loose ends of the play.

Comedy probably arose from country festivals in celebration of the vine. Rowdy revellers, bearing torches and holding aloft a phallic emblem, and accompanied by musicians, caroused from village to village. These bands were called *comedus*, and their songs called *comoedia*, or comedy.

The tragedies and comedies of the ancient Pagan Greeks remain fresh and fascinating to this day, and are performed by high school drama departments and the world's best theater companies.

See **Isis and Osiris, Dionysus, Masks, Aristophanes.**

42

Writing

From as far back as 50,000 B.C.E., early peoples carved primitive hash marks on stone, bone, and wood to count and keep track of days and nights and lunations. True writing, in which inscriptions convey sound and meaning, rather than merely pictographs, seems to have arisen independently in three different parts of the paleo-Pagan world. The oldest, from ancient Sumeria (now Iraq) around 3200 B.C.E., was called cuneiform, meaning "wedge-writing." The wedge-shaped incisions—representing objects, people, and animals—were made on wet clay tablets. Trained scribes performed this task using a blunt reed called a stylus. Only a minority of people, from the ruling class and theocracy, learned to read and write. They employed professional scribes who, due to their value and use to the ruling classes, were privy to their secrets. As pictographs evolved into symbols for specific sounds rather than icons of objects, animals, and people, they gradually became stylized and lost their iconographic forms. This transition from icon to sound symbol

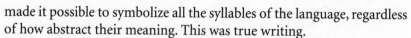

made it possible to symbolize all the syllables of the language, regardless of how abstract their meaning. This was true writing.

The first document in history was a bill of lading. Writing technology on parchment or clay signaled the dawn of the information revolution. Writing facilitated economic and political expansion, as well as the need to record new places, names, and abstract thoughts. Writing was used in commerce to keep inventory and assess taxes. The invention of writing allowed for the diffusion of news and ideas to distant places without reliance on a messenger with a good memory. Writing soon came to be used for spiritual, historical, and cultural reasons. Some of the greatest literary works in history, such as the Epic of Gilgamesh and the Descent of Inanna, were recorded in Sumerian cuneiform script.

The idea of writing became diffused to many parts of Southwest Asia, and to Egypt, Crete, and Elam (east of Sumer in present-day southwestern Iran), where clay inscriptions date back to 2500 B.C.E. The principle of using symbols for sound appears in the Indus Valley in what is now Pakistan. Texts written on bark from Afghanistan or Pakistan have recently come to light in the British Library. They apparently contain the first known Buddhist text; the Gautama Buddha died in 456 B.C.E., yet no Buddhist writings precede the seventh century C.E.

The best known early writing is found in Egyptian hieroglyphs, meaning holy writing. Hieroglyphs, dating from about 3100 B.C.E., were carved with a knife on ivory or bone, or they used ochre and carbon to ink writings on papyrus, leather, or linen. There were three kinds of ancient Egyptian writing systems: hieroglyphics were carved into stone for religious or ceremonial uses; cursive hieratic script was preferred for drawing, writing letters, and for accounting purposes because it was easiest to use; and demotic (popular, colloquial) was a standardized shorthand for even faster writing. Coptic writing superseded hieroglyphics around 300 C.E. when Egyptians converted to Christianity and earlier writing was banned.

The locus of the third primary independent evidence of writing is found in northern China during the Shang dynasty, 1200–1045 B.C.E., considerably later than cuneiform. Later but still Pagan, the Olmecs of present-day Mexico developed a syllabic system of glyphs around 400 B.C.E. This system was improved by the Maya and was in use from 200 C.E. until the Spanish conquest in the early sixteenth century. Olmec and Mayan writing was limited to the priestly ruling class to record significant ecclesiastical writings. (Other early forms of writing from the Pagan world include runic writing among the Germanic peoples and Ogham among the Celts.)

In today's world, much of the population assumes literacy as its right, enjoying books, newspapers, magazines, and reading on the World Wide Web—a comfortable place for NeoPagans.

See **Papyrus, Parchment/Vellum, and Paper, Leather and Tanning, Libraries, Encyclopedia, The Descent of Inanna, The *Epic of Gilgamesh*, The Witches' Voice.**

III

PEOPLE

All the entries in this section are people who actually lived, and all made significant contributions to society and culture. They include poets and playwrights, philosophers and politicians, mathematicians, artists and warriors. Some are so widely known they are taken almost for granted; others are very obscure but their work was important. See how many of them you recognize.

43

Aristophanes

The work of the comic poet named Aristophanes is as fresh and topical today as it was when it was written more than two thousand years ago in ancient Greece. His plays have been performed repeatedly from the time they were first written until today. The playwright Aristophanes lived from circa 446 to 385 B.C.E., and was educated in Athens.

The Peloponnesian War, roughly 431–404 B.C.E. between Athens and Sparta, was being waged in Aristophanes' time. One of his earlier surviving works is the world's first anti-war comedy. Written in the sixth year of the war, *The Acharnians* was sparked by the poet's concern for the suffering of the rural population of Attica, the area surrounding Athens that was exposed to continual invasions. He must have been quite a man about town, because his plays frequently dealt with current political situations with biting and hilarious satire. For instance, in his play *The Knights* Aristophanes mocked the bloated and alcoholic countenance of the Athenian tyrant Cleon, successor to Pericles; the writer himself played the character of Cleon, portrayed as a tanner, because no one else dared. So incisive were his plays that prominent figures who took offense at his humor sometimes prosecuted him and his sponsors in the courts of law. He wrote comedies for the two annual Athenian festivals, the Dionysia (described more fully elsewhere in this book), and the Lenea. His plays were eagerly awaited and well attended by the people of Athens.

One of Aristophanes' best-known plays, written in 441 B.C.E., for the festival of Dionysus, is called *The Birds* (in Greek, *Ornithes*). In this play, birds act as a chorus to talk directly to the audience. They speak of the ridiculousness of human beings keeping birds as pets in cages, the perversion of cooking and eating them, and the great importance of birds in the universe. They speak from a place with the comical name of "Cloud-cuckooland." Without mocking any individual person, *The Birds* illustrates the corruption and greediness Aristophanes saw in Athenian society.

The comedies *The Birds*, *The Wasps*, *Lysistrata*, and *The Frogs*, which concerns a visit by the god Dionysus disguised as the demigod Heracles and accompanied by the chorus of frogs as he is ferried across the water to Hades' Underworld, are among the eleven surviving plays of the thirty that Aristophanes wrote. His plays are the only extant examples of a school of theater called Old Greek Comedy.

In his ribald comedy *Lysistrata*, Aristophanes makes a compelling pacifist statement. The women in the play withhold their sexual favors from the belligerent men until the men cease warmongering. It continues to be performed to this day, even inspiring the twentieth-century Spanish painter Pablo Picasso to create a series of paintings based on it.

In January 2003 people all over the world held readings of *Lysistrata* in their local communities in protest of the pending U.S. invasion of Iraq.

See **Theater.**

44

Asclepius

Asclepius [also spelled *Aesculapius, Aesclepius, Asklepios* (Latin: *Aesculapius*)] is one of those mysterious figures who was a living person but who became what is called "euhemerized." That is, his influence was so profound that he grew to the stature of legend and from thence into a divine figure. Asclepius is the Greek, and later Roman, god of healing.

For a mortal, Asclepius seems to have had semidivine origins, since his mother was the nymph Coronis, a princess of Thessaly, and his father the god Apollo. Coronis died (or was killed) when Asclepius was an infant and Apollo entrusted him to the centaur (half man, half horse) Chiron. Chiron taught the child all the arts of healing. The centaur's young student grew to become a skilled healer, with knowledge of drugs, herbs, and incantations. He also performed surgery and healed some ailments with his hands alone, using touch and manipulation. Word of Asclepius's prodigious skills spread throughout Greece.

Asclepius's family was also considered to have healing powers, most notably his daughter Hygeia ("healing"), from whose name we get our English word hygiene, meaning cleanliness. His other daughter was Panacea ("all healing" or "all remedy").

People erected many temples and shrines dedicated to Asclepius in Thessaly, Cos, and elsewhere. Called Asclepions, these temples were maintained by priest healers, who used snakes and ointments in their healing work. The species of snake became known as Asclepion snakes; they were said to foster healing by licking the patients. The sick came from near and far to the Ascelpions to pray and seek cures for their illnesses. Some patients brought sacrifices and gifts of goods and money. Many even stayed overnight to receive dream visitations by Asclepius; in the morning priests interpreted the dreams and administered treatments according to those interpretations. As an extension of the Ascelpions, people established medical schools.

The symbol for Asclepius was the serpent, specifically an Asclepion snake, wrapped around a staff, a symbol still used today. The active worship of Asclepius lasted for about seventeen hundred years, from circa 1200 B.C.E. through circa 500 C.E. His cult was prevalent right up until the end of the Roman Empire. Today Asclepius is still worshipped and revered by contemporary twenty-first-century C.E. Pagans.

See **Hippocrates, Caduceus.**

45

Boudica

Boudica (also spelled, variously, Boadicea, Bunduica, Voadicia, Bonducca, Boudicca, or Boudicea and meaning in the Celtic tongue of the day "Victory") was born about 25 C.E. into the Trinovante tribe. By the time of the Roman invasion of Britain in 43 C.E., she ruled, with her husband, Prasutagus, as queen of the Iceni, a Celtic tribe living in Norfolk and Suffolk in eastern England. During this time the Iceni had prospered due to flourishing trade with the Roman Empire, because Prasutagus was a Roman client, and the king and queen had amassed riches and power.

An account of the day by the Roman Cassius Dio describes Boudica's appearance: "In stature she was very tall, in appearance most terrifying, in the glance of her eye most fierce, and her voice was harsh; a great mass of the tawniest hair fell to her hips; around her neck was a large golden necklace; and she wore a tunic of divers colours over which a thick mantle was fastened with a brooch. This was her invariable attire."

After Prasutagus's death, however, relations between the invaders and the native Britons changed. Roman women did not enjoy the high status in Roman society that their Celtic sisters held, so the Romans could not accept the rule of Prasutagus's widow. When tensions mounted, the Roman centurions (soldiers) pillaged the house, plundered their possessions, and raped Boudica's two daughters. Boudica and the Iceni people were humiliated. Boudica was whipped: "her body seamed with ignominious stripes" (meaning she was whipped), according to the Roman historian Tacitus. The Romans drove the natives from their lands, treated them cruelly, hurled insults at them, and made the Iceni and other local Celtic tribes a subject population. The proud, independent-minded, liberty-loving Iceni did not accept subjugation to the Romans. Such a condition went against their nature. Boudica, enjoined by the Trinobantians and other neighboring tribes, rallied her people to revolt. These rebels met in secret and pledged themselves to the cause of liberty.

This revolt culminated in battle. Boudica rode her chariot through the ranks of outraged Celts, shouting: "This is not the first time that the Britons have been led to battle by a woman . . . From the pride and arrogance of the Romans nothing is sacred; all are subject to violation; the old endure the scourge, and the virgins are deflowered. But the vindictive gods are now at hand. . . . Look round, and view your numbers. Behold the proud display of warlike spirits, and consider the motives for which we draw the avenging sword. On this spot we must either conquer, or die with glory. There is no alternative. Though a woman, my resolution is fixed: the men, if they please, may survive with infamy, and live in bondage."

The Celtic warriors were wild and undisciplined, unlike the well-organized and well-equipped Roman legions. During the revolt, which lasted for several months in 60–61 C.E., the Iceni and their allies burned and destroyed Londinium (London), Verulamium (St. Albans), and Camulodunum (Colchester). Despite the rightness of their cause, their bravery, and their ferocity, the Britons ultimately succumbed to the more disciplined Roman army and took flight. Contemporary observers estimated that eighty thousand Celts were put to the sword, while the Romans lost only about four hundred men. Rather than live in ignominy and subjection, Boudica took poison and ended her life.

During the long reign of Queen Victoria in the nineteenth century, the British erected a great bronze statue of Boudica and her daughters, standing behind rearing horses in her war chariot, at Westminster Bridge across from the Houses of Parliament. Today, modern feminists look upon Boudica as a martyr and a model of a woman standing up for herself and her people. The Pagan Boudica has an honored place on the altars of Witches and Celtic Reconstructionists alike.

46

Cumaean Sybil

With the exception of the Oracle at Delphi in Greece, the Sybil at Cumae, near what is now Naples, Italy, is the best-known ancient seeress. The Sybil was not an immortal, although when Aeneas met her on his journey, she was said to have been seven hundred years old. The god Apollo had once fancied her and she had spurned his advances. Thus Apollo tried to bribe her with the promise of immortality, to which the Sybil replied that she wanted as many years of life as there were grains of sand in a nearby pile—but she forgot to mention Youth. Thereupon, Apollo left her to become prey to the ravages of Old Age.

Cumae was at a shrine dedicated to Apollo within a grove sacred to his sister, the goddess Artemis. The temple itself had been built by the master architect Daedalus, the same man who designed the Trojan Horse and the labyrinth at Minos. It contained sculptures and its walls were adorned with reliefs depicting Cretan events. Like many oracular sites, Cumae was an area that produced unusual geothermal phenomena, such as mephitic (from the Latin *mephistis*, an area where foul-smelling poisonous gases arise from within the earth) emanations called "Plutonia," named for the Roman Underworld god Pluto, cognate with the Greek Hades. A Plutonium was regarded as a place where there was an entrance to the Underworld. So it is to Cumae that both the Trojan Aeneas and the Greek Odysseus travel in order to reach Hades.

Aeneas arrives at this place where the Sybil hears voices and gives prophecy, and sacrifices seven bullocks to the god, as prescribed, and addresses his wishes to Apollo. The Sybil, with wild hair, heaving breast, and foaming mouth, becomes possessed by the god, and thus delivers her oracle to Aeneas about his future in Lavinium, an ancient Latin town. Aeneas, however, protests that he learned nothing new or unexpected, and he boldly asks the prophetess to guide him to the Underworld. The Sybil explains the danger of such a venture, and instructs him to get a particular magical Golden Bough as an offering for Persephone, the Underworld Queen. This bough is in a hidden dell in the woods. No sword can hew it; only one who is fated can pluck it easily from the tree. Now Aeneas is a son of the goddess Aphrodite, so at this turn of events he turns to his mother for help. Aphrodite sends two of her sacred doves to lead Aeneas to the tree they settle upon. The Golden Bough breaks off with a single pull.

Back at the cave, the Sybil pours libations and calls upon the goddess Hekate for help in their journey. Aeneas sets up an altar to Hades and makes sacrifices to Persephone, Gaia, and Nyx, mother of night and unseen spirits. In the darkness of night, the ground begins to rumble and the howling of hounds are heard as Hekate approaches to open the way.

Aeneas and the Sybil step into the Underworld, where they encounter all manner of fearsome creatures—disease and hunger, grief and discord. Eventually the filthy Charon ferries the two across the River Styx, where the Sybil calms the ferocious, two-headed dog, Cerebus, with honey cake infused with a sedative potion. Finally the two journeyers arrive at the Palace of Hades in Elysium, the abode of the blessed dead. There, Aeneas places the Golden Bough at Persephone's doorway. And there, although Aeneas is unable to embrace the shade of his dead father Anchises, he is able to converse with him about all manner of things. When they eventually return to the world of the living, Aeneas is so grateful for the Sybil's help that he swears to "erect a temple to you and there burn incense in your honour" (Ovid, *Metamorphoses*).

Although the Sybil herself is long gone, she has left spiritual daughters and sons throughout contemporary Pagandom who seek prophetic visions in wild, sacred places, and who venture into unknown depths of Earth.

See **Aphrodite, Hekate, Oracles and Seers, Delphic Oracle, The *Aenead* Ovid.**

47

Enheduanna

Enheduanna is the world's oldest known author. Her works, written in cuneiform on clay tablets, were composed approximately 4,300 years ago. She lived, composed, and taught roughly 2,000 years before philosopher and teacher Aristotle and the poet Homer, 1,700 years before the Greek poet Sappho, and 800 years before the Epic of Gilgamesh.

Enheduanna's best-known surviving works are hymns to the goddess Inanna. She composed both lyrics and music to her hymns, which were sung to the accompaniment of a stringed instrument, probably a lyre, harp, or lute, all of which were in use in her culture. In fact, ancient clay tablets from the ancient Assyrian and Babylonian cultures (circa 2800 B.C.E.) and written in the dead Semitic languages of Akkadian and Hurrian contain musical notations and instructions that allow modern archaeo-musicologists to reconstruct their scales and tuning systems.

Enheduanna lived in what is today Iraq during the Old Akkadian time period circa 2300–2225 B.C.E. Her mother was a Sumerian from southern Mesopotamia and her father, Sardor the Great, was an Akkadian from the north. He was the first ruler to unite northern and southern Mesopotamia, from his capital city of Ur, into what is now Iraq.

Sardor appointed his talented, educated, strong-minded daughter, the princess Enheduanna, as "*en*," or high priestess. Surviving images of Enheduanna show her wearing a rolled-brim turban, called the *aga*, indicative of *en*-ship, and the flounced dress of the priestess. The second part of her name, "*heduana*," refers to the moon god Nanna, the "ornament of heaven," whose priestess Enheduanna was. As priestess to Nanna, Enheduanna was the early representative of his romantic partner, the goddess Inanna. She stands at the threshold of heaven and Earth, communicating between the two.

The *ens* lived in temple complexes comprised of a temple, the private residential quarters of the priestess, a kitchen, a dining area, and the cemetery where dead *en*-priestesses were buried and to whom periodic offerings were made. Two significant holy objects within the temple complex were the drums and the ovens.

The writings of Enheduanna portray the feminine as powerfully equal, necessary, and valuable to her people and culture. In her hymns, she moves from the third person to the first person, displaying a strong authorial presence unmatched in the ancient world. She sings of birth and death, creation and destruction. Enheduanna's life was one of a fully realized woman, one concerned with things that occupy the deepest part of the psyche, showing individuality as well as a strong sense of community.

Just as her father Sardor united northern and southern Mesopotamia, Enheduanna, in her passionately complex hymns to the goddess Inanna, unites the warlike qualities of Akkadian Ishtar with those gentler qualities of love and fecundity of Sumerian Inanna.

Pagans, feminists, historians, and artists see in this woman who lived many centuries ago a valuable model of an accomplished and self-actualized woman. Let us hope that Enheduanna's example and Inanna's grace lend strength, stamina, integrity, and eventual peace to the discord-plagued lands from which they arose.

See **Drums and Drumming, Baking and Ovens, Lipushau**

48

Marija Gimbutas

Marija Gimbutas, one of the most controversial thinkers of the twentieth century, was given a full state funeral, complete with Romuva Pagan priests and attended by thousands, in her home city of Vilnius when she died in 1994. This was the city where her parents had established the first Lithuanian hospital and a Montessori school. Her mother Veronika and her aunt were the first two female physicians in Northeastern Europe. Marija was born in 1921 to a mother who was an occultist as well as a medical doctor and a father who was a writer, folklorist, and physician.

When she first entered university, Marija studied linguistics, although she had previously participated in ethnographic expeditions. Greatly affected by the Lithuanian peasantry and their relationship with the land, and distressed at the Polish occupiers' prohibition on speaking the Lithuanian language, Marija collected at least five thousand folksongs from among the refugees from Byelorussia, as Russia expanded and World War II loomed. In 1941 she joined the underground resistance movement, and shortly thereafter Russia began arrests, deportations, and executions of the resistors. Twenty-five members of Marija's family disappeared in June of that year.

By the end of June Germany had attacked Russia and occupied Lithuania, but in the midst of this Marija Alseika and Jurgis Gimbutas had fallen in love and married. Within three years, the Soviets had taken over Lithuania and the young family—for by now Marija and Jurgis had a daughter—were forced to flee. They fled by raft, train, and over the Alps by bicycle, to find respite in Tubingen, Germany. There, Marija received her doctor of philosophy degree, gave birth to another daughter, and published her thesis. In 1947 the family immigrated to the United States, where, in 1950, Marija began translating ancient text and studying the warriors and weapons of Bronze Age Europe at Harvard University. By 1955 she was named Research Fellow of Harvard's Peabody Museum (a lifetime honor).

In 1956, Marija first presented her "Kurgan Hypothesis" at an international conference in Philadelphia. She called the Proto-Indo-European–speaking peoples who flourished throughout Neolithic Europe (between 6500 and 3500 B.C.E.) Kurgans because of their distinctive burial mounds. Marija was intrigued by the fact that these peoples left thousands of female figures in art and pottery, but no evidence of warfare prior to Indo-European influence. In her Kurgan Hypothesis, Marija was the first to bridge academic disciplines by bringing together mythological, folkloric, linguistic, and archaeological knowledge to discover the origins and trace the migrations of these peoples.

By the time Marija accepted an appointment at the University of California at Los Angeles in 1963, she had published several books and numerous articles and had lectured throughout the world. Throughout the 1960s and '70s, Marija directed excavations of Neolithic sites in Yugoslavia, particularly Macedonia. She also received prestigious academic awards as well as the 1968 L.A. Times Woman of the Year Award.

In 1981 Marija returned to the USSR with the American Academy of Sciences on a Fulbright fellowship. When she lectured at Vilnius University, she said, "[t]here is an organization now, sort of a pagan organization which indirectly was influenced by my being there or my writings. They are called Romuva, which is the name of a sacred hill and also described as a sanctuary in the fourteenth century. So this is the name for this reawakening of pagan rituals."

This ancient spirituality is now an official religion in Lithuania. Many American Pagans are Romuva too. In addition to inspiring and being inspired by contemporary Romuva Pagans, Marija's works, particularly *The Goddesses and Gods of Old Europe*, *The Language of the Goddess*, and *The Civilization of the Goddess*, have influenced the women's spirituality community, Dianic and other Witches, artists, poets, philosophers, and social thinkers. Her vision of a peaceful, egalitarian earth-based spirituality strikes a deep chord in Pagan hearts. The year 2004 sees the release of a film biography of Marija, narrated by her good friend, actress Olympia Dukakis.

See **Prehistoric "Venus" Figurines.**

49

Hippocrates

Hippocrates was the greatest physician of antiquity. He is regarded as the father of medicine, and one of the most outstanding figures in medicine of all time.

He was born in 460 B.C.E. in Kos, Greece, where his physician father taught him medicine. From there he traveled, and probably studied medicine for some time in Athens before he returned to Kos and founded a medical school called the Asclepium of Kos. Hippocrates acquired immense knowledge of natural science, including chemistry, physics, and biology, as demonstrated by the sixty or seventy treatises he wrote. Among them were treatises on medical history, fractures, hemorrhoids, head injuries, epidemics, embryology, surgery, and ulcers. He advocated a methodology that relied on observation and querying of the patient as well as physical examination of the patient. He also considered the physician to be a servant of nature.

Hippocrates was the first to accurately describe symptoms of pneumonia. He also had an inkling of the genetic predisposition of diseases within families and over successive generations, before genetics were known. In addition, in *Regimen* and *Regimen in Acute Diseases*, Hippocrates wrote about preventive medicine, and he maintained that proper diet and lifestyle can prevent disease and can help a patient recover from illness.

Hippocrates' innovative theories are set forth in his many writings. In three works —*Prognostic, Coan Prognosis,* and *Aphorisms*—he posits that by observing enough cases, a physician can predict the course of a disease. His *Sacred Disease* is a treatise on epilepsy. Later, in *Airs, Waters, and Places*, Hippocrates discusses the environmental causes of disease instead of attributing them to divine origin, for at the time disease was commonly considered to have been divine in origin; he also considers weather and drinking water as factors.

Hippocrates is thought to have written the Hippocratic Oath, which is still sworn by physicians today. By the words of the preamble to the Oath, we can see that Hippocrates was a Pagan—"I swear by Apollo the physician, by Aesculapius, Hygeia and Panacea, and I take to witness all the gods, all the goddesses, to keep according to my ability and my judgment, the following Oath." The substance of the oath pledges the physician to work for the good of the patient, to do him or her no harm, to prescribe no deadly drugs, and to keep confidential medical information regarding the patient.

Other time-honored quotes from Hippocrates are "Walking is man's best medicine" and "*Primum non nocere,*" "First, do no harm." Like any modern spellworker, Hippocrates maintained that "Prayer indeed is good, but while calling on the gods a man should himself lend a hand."

The great physician died in 377 B.C.E., his rich legacy having been borne out over the centuries since he was active. Hippocrates continues to serve as a worthy role model for both healers and Pagans.

See **Caduceus, Asclepius.**

50

Homer

We know that Homer was a blind court singer and storyteller whose profession probably involved much travel around the lands surrounding the Aegean Sea. Not much is known of Homer as a person, but he left us two epic works, the *Iliad* and the *Odyssey*. He was said to have sung ten epic poems about the Trojan War, but only these two survive. The *Iliad* tells of the war itself, and the *Odyssey* tells of Odysseus's return from Troy. Some scholars attribute their composition to several individuals. Homer's writings are the most important literary source for knowledge of this period. In them, the poet combines history, religion, myth, and lore of many generations.

Modern scholars hold different opinions as to when Homer lived. Some believe he lived at the beginning of the twelfth century B.C.E. around the time of the Trojan War, while others believe that he wrote three hundred years later. Scholars who maintain this second position believe that Homer composed his tales of the conflict between the Mycenaeans and the Trojans from poetry passed down from storyteller to storyteller over the intervening generations. Regardless of which theory is correct, all agree that Homer's epic poems are among the most important texts to emerge from ancient Greek culture. In them, the poet articulates the values, ethics, and worldview of the basic Greek character, thus creating the defining moment in the formation of the Greek national and cultural identity.

The age in which Homer lived and wrote is called, variously, the Homeric, the Heroic, the Myceneaen, or the Late Minoan Age. Society was tribal in nature, and patriarchal, although women of the time participated in athletic competitions and enjoyed freedom and status denied to them in later Greek society. Slaves, who were mostly females captured in war, and hired men performed the necessary drudge work, while the noblemen pursued such activities as hunting, herding livestock, and fighting. These men enthusiastically enjoyed the pleasures of hospitality—good food, wine, camaraderie, and entertainment, especially the chanting of the bard.

A ruler, called a *basileis*, chosen from among the nobility served as king, general, judge, and religious officiant. However, he did not have absolute power; rather, the basileis was assisted by an advisory council composed of noblemen called *aristoi*, meaning "the best." This is the root of the modern English word "aristocrat." Achilles, the hero of the *Iliad*, in combining nobility of action, mind, and honor, represents the heroic ideal. Although many people today do not hold the same ideals, Achilles' choice of a short, heroic life of fame and glory over a long, happy life was completely understandable to his contemporaries.

In the *Odyssey*, the main character, Odysseus, the "man of many ways" or "man of many tricks," is a more pragmatic hero; he stays the course on his return home despite overwhelming obstacles and temptations. The poem deals with the nature of human civilization and human savagery. Homer's stories show that an honorable man proves his honor (*arete*) in peacetime by excelling in athletics, and in war with his military skill, prowess, and courage. Homer's poems continue to inspire paintings, plays, novels, television shows, and films, such as *Oh, Brother, Where Art Thou?* His characters, their foibles, interactions, and strange adventures appeal to people across the ages.

See **The *Iliad*, The *Odyssey*.**

51

Hypatia

Hypatia of Alexandria was a remarkable woman not only for her own time, but for any time. She was an independent woman of prodigious intellect who went on to establish herself as a thinker, an inventor, and a teacher. Born in the late fourth century C.E. in Egypt, Hypatia learned philosophy and mathematics, astronomy and astrology from her father,

Theon, the last head of the Alexandria Museum. Theon also instilled in Hypatia respect for her body by encouraging regular vigorous exercise for physical and mental health. Under his tutelage, she studied the different religions of the world as well as the art of oration. Concerning the matter of world religions, Hypatia said, "All formal dogmatic religions are fallacious and must never be accepted by self-respecting persons as final." Such a sentiment resonates in the hearts of NeoPagans, most of whom have a distinct aversion to dogma of any kind. She admonishes people to "Reserve your right to think, for even to think wrongly is better than not to think at all."

Hypatia grew to become a powerful orator, much admired by her colleagues and students alike. She is described as having been a charismatic teacher who attracted students, including many prominent Christians, from other cities. One of her most prominent Christian students was Synesius of Cyrene, later the bishop of Ptolemais. Surviving letters from him to her tell how greatly Synesius admired Hypatia's superior knowledge and intellect.

Hypatia's writings consist of three major treatises on geometry and algebra and one on astronomy. She edited a book on conics, making the geometrical concepts of hyperbolas, parabolas, and ellipses easier to understand. Unfortunately, none of Hypatia's writings have survived except for the titles and references to them. Her writings included extensive correspondence with people she knew from her travels throughout the Mediterranean. In addition to writing books, Hypatia is credited with having invented an astrolabe, an instrument for measuring the specific gravity of water, another for distilling water, and a planisphere, a map formed by the projection of a sphere or part of a sphere on a plane, especially an adjustable circular star map that shows the appearance of the heavens at a specific time and place.

The Alexandrian political scene during Hypatia's time was filled with discord, as dogmatic Christians, following a decree from the emperor Theodosius in Rome, sought to eradicate Paganism. The appointment of Cyril in 412 C.E. to the ecclesiastical office of patriarch of Alexandria exacerbated this power struggle between church and state. His rival was the Roman prefect, Orestes, civil governor of the city. The fact that Hypatia was both female and Pagan antagonized those who would impose Christianity on all residents. She was too uppity, in their conservative viewpoint. The political climate became increasingly tense, with frequent riots between dogmatic Christians on the one side and Pagans and tolerant Christians on the other. Hypatia sided with her friend Orestes. Probably due to someone having spread virulent rumors about her, in 415 a group of Nitrian monks, fanatical Christians and supporters of Cyril, attacked and brutally murdered Hypatia. According to reports, the mob stripped her naked and beat her, then dragged her through the city to a church. While she was still alive, they tore away her flesh with oyster shells or pottery shards. Then they burned her remains.

In an account written three centuries later, John, Bishop of Nikiu, describes Hypatia as "the pagan woman who had beguiled the people of the city and the prefect through her enchantments." He called her a witch, saying, "she was devoted at all times to magic, astrolabes and instruments of music, and she beguiled many people through (her) Satanic [*sic*] wiles."

Such authors as Voltaire, the astronomer Carl Sagan, and the historian Edward Gibbon have used Hypatia's death as a symbol of the repression of reason by irrational religion. To me, Hypatia is a Pagan martyr.

52

Charles Godfrey Leland

Charles Godfrey Leland, an American author, lawyer, humorist, and journalist, wrote a provocative and controversial book about Italian Witches. Called *Aradia, or the Gospel of the Witches*, this book, first published in 1899 but still in print today, was an early contribution to the emerging field of folklore.

Born in Philadelphia in August 1824, Leland was the son of a prosperous mercantile family, with its attendant advantages of education. His lifelong fascination with magic and folklore began in early childhood, sparked by tales of the *sidhe* (fairies) told to him by an immigrant Irish housemaid, and the Voodoo he learned from an African kitchen servant. Throughout his life, he carried charms and amulets in his pockets. After being graduated from Princeton University in 1845, Leland studied at the universities of Heidelberg and Munich, and at the Sorbonne. While in Paris, he took an active part in the Revolution of 1848. Leland returned to Philadelphia, where he was admitted to the bar in 1851, and thereafter began working as a journalist and editor. He published an abolitionist periodical in Boston called the *Continental Magazine*. After the Civil War, Leland traveled throughout the American West, eventually marrying a woman named Isabel. During this time Leland wrote several volumes of humor and dialect poems, collectively known as *Hans Breitmann's Ballads*, burlesquing German Americans.

The couple moved to England in 1870, where Leland's fascination with folklore led him to study the English Gypsies. He learned to speak their Romany language, later published well-regarded books—*The English Gypsies and Their Language* (1872), *The Gypsies* (1882), and *Gypsy Sorcery and Fortunetelling*—and in 1888 became the first president of the Gypsy-Lore Society. Among Leland's other folklore titles are *Algonquin Legends of New England* and *Songs of the Sea and Lays of the Land*. He went on to serve as president of the first European folklore congress, held in Paris in 1889.

While living in Florence, Leland wrote *Etruscan Roman Remains* and *Legends of Florence*. It was there that he met Maddalena, a fortuneteller who claimed to be a hereditary Witch, born into a "witch family" from Romagna Toscana. Her grandmother, aunt, and especially her stepmother taught Maddalena how to prepare enchanted medicines, philters, or spells, and brought her up to believe in her destiny as a sorceress. They taught her to chant in strange prescribed tones, incantations or evocations to the ancient gods of Italy. As an adult, Maddalena and her colleagues, followers of the goddess Diana, practiced a form of Italian Witchcraft called *stregheria*. Around 1888, Maddalena initiated Leland into the "Witch-Lore of the Romagna." Leland's writings are the source of much of what we know today of Italian Witchcraft.

The old folklorist died in Florence in 1903, leaving a heritage of Witch lore and liturgy that predated the books of the better-known British Witch, Gerald Brousseau Gardner, by more than fifty years.

53

Lipushau

Lipushau is the first named drummer in history. Beyond that fact, little is known about her, but that alone, and especially since she was a woman, makes her worthy of inclusion here. Lipushau lived in Mesopotamia (present-day Iraq) around 2380 B.C.E., where she was High Priestess in the city-state of Ur. Her official title was "*en*," which means "high priestess." Like her grand-aunt Enheduanna, Lipushau was a priestess of the moon god Nanna, and she presided at Nanna's temple, called the Eki-

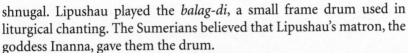

shnugal. Lipushau played the *balag-di*, a small frame drum used in liturgical chanting. The Sumerians believed that Lipushau's matron, the goddess Inanna, gave them the drum.

Lipushau was the granddaughter of King Naram-Sin, who, himself, was the grandson of Sargon the Great, the first to unite Northern and Southern Mesopotamia. Incidentally, the story of baby Sargon, though earlier, is nearly identical to the story of Moses as a baby. Sargon's mother was supposedly a priestess who gave birth in secret and then put Sargon in an ark of bullrushes lined with pitch and released it to the river. The river brought the little boat to the notice of a gardener, who took Sargon home and raised him as his son. As Sargon grew older, he became the cupbearer to the king of Kish. He later broke with him and established his own city, Ur. He had five children; Enheduanna, High Priestess and author of the earliest known epic poems, was his only daughter.

Though Lipushau is little known today, the acknowledgment of her profession and status in the ancient world inspires pride in today's women—particularly Pagan women and particularly women who drum. The magic of the drum cannot be overstated. A contemporary Pagan women's frame-drum group in Los Angeles have named themselves Lipushau and perform in her honor.

See **Drums and Drumming, Enheduanna.**

54

Ovid

Pagans owe a huge debt of gratitude to the Roman poet Ovid. To call him simply a poet is to understate Ovid's lasting influence on Western art, thought, and story. His greatest work, *Metamorphoses*, written in 8 C.E., rivaled the Bible in popularity among readers of the Middle Ages (fifth to fifteenth centuries) and the Renaissance (fourteenth through seventeenth centuries).

Born in Sulmo, in central Italy, in 43 B.C.E., just a year after the assassination of Julius Caesar, to a relatively well-off family, Ovid (full name Publius Ovidius Naso) was educated in Rome for a career in law. He soon turned to his true calling, poetry, under the patronage of a patrician orator, soldier, and linguist named M. Valerius Messalla Corvinus. Ovid was reading his work to appreciative listeners before he was twenty and grew to become Rome's most popular and celebrated poet by age thirty.

Ovid's considerable poetic output, always witty and sophisticated, displayed irreverence moving into subtle parody. His work contrasted with that of his older, more staid contemporaries, Horace and Vergil. Ovid was concerned with women, love, and the changes brought about by love of all kinds. His most important work, *Metamorphoses*, is our premier classical source of 250 myths, including the hubris of Icarus in thinking he could fly to Jupiter's various erotic dalliances with Io, Callisto, and Europa.

Ovid lived at a time in Roman history when the older republican form of government was being superseded. Julius Caesar's nephew Octavian disapproved of Antony's relationship with the Egyptian queen Cleopatra, so he banished them to Actium and declared himself Emperor Augustus. Ovid's upbringing in a time of relative peace and prosperity parallels the rearing of children in post–World War II America in the 1950s and '60s. He had not known much of privation and struggle. So while the Senate, dominated by an emperor filled with reformist zeal, passed ever more conservative legislation attempting to regulate morals, Ovid and his contemporaries rebelled and lived a life full of fun and erotic escapades. He has been called "the playboy of the Roman world."

When Ovid was fifty, Augustus exiled him to the remote garrison town of Tomi, on the Black Sea in what is now Romania. For a sophisticated urban fellow like Ovid, being forced to live in the barren hinterlands so distant from Rome must have been an extreme punishment. The reason for Ovid's exile is not known, but it happened suddenly. Scholars speculate that Ovid had incurred such extreme displeasure in the emperor due, in part, to Ovid's friendship with Augustus's recalcitrant granddaughter Julia. Julia had been passed around to various husbands for political alliances, and later in life rebelled and lived a freer and perhaps more dissolute life than patrician Roman women were allowed. The other offense seems to be Ovid's *Ars Amatoria* (*The Book of Love*), about adultery.

Whatever the reasons, Ovid was unhappy in Tomi. His literary output from that period portrays melancholy and despair, as evidenced by his last work, *Tristia* (*Sorrows*). Although he attempted to regain his former favor with Augustus by writing *Fasti*, a poetic treatment of the Roman festival calendar and legends relating to each, he ultimately failed. Ovid died in Tomi about nine years after his exile.

In later times, such esteemed writers as Dante, Chaucer, Milton, Spenser, and W. H. Auden have found in Ovid a major inspiration. Christopher Marlowe draws from the story of Daedalus and Icarus in his tragedy *Dr. Faustus*. Shakespeare's *Romeo and Juliet* is taken from Ovid's poem about the doomed lovers Pyramus and Thisbe.

55

Sappho

The great Greek lyrist Sappho, one of few known female poets in the ancient world, was born circa 615 B.C.E. in pre-classical Greece (circa 750–490 B.C.E.). Her father, Scamandrnymus, was a prominent citizen of Mitylene on the island of Lesbos. Her mother was Clis and she had two brothers—Charaxus and Larichus. The latter served as public cup-bearer at Mitlene; since only well-born youths were eligible for this role, this fact provides further evidence of the status of Sappho's family. Scamandrnymus died when Sappho was six. Whether or not Sappho married a wealthy merchant from the island of Andros is a subject of dispute among scholars, but it is certain that Sappho had an adored daughter named Cleis.

Sappho traveled widely, settling for a time in Sicily. When she came to live in their city, the residents of Syracuse erected a bronze statue of her. She is described as having been small and dark in appearance, with bright, intelligent eyes exuding charm and grace. Numerous illustrations of Sappho appear on Greek vases.

The seventh century B.C.E. was a time of cultural growth and change in many places in the Mediterranean and Near East. Concurrent with Aeolian culture of which the island of Lesbos was the center, the biblical Jeremiah began to prophesy (628), Daniel was abducted to Babylon (607), and Nebuchadnezzar conquered Jerusalem (587). Also around that time the Greek alphabet came into use, coin money was minted, and the arts flourished. In fact, crude coins bearing Sappho's image were minted in Lesbos during her lifetime.

Compared with their Greek contemporaries, the Dorians and the Ionians, the Aeolians showed a fierce and passionate temperament. Ionian women of the time were confined in harems; Spartan women lived rigorously disciplined lives. But the Lesbian ladies enjoyed uncommon social and domestic freedom. They were educated and cultivated, and unafraid to express their feelings and opinions. They had the freedom to be who and what they wanted to be.

In this fertile cultural environment, amid the flowers and fruits, sweet scents and birdsong of the lush valley of Lesbos, Sappho was part of a new wave of Greek lyrists. These young poets changed point of view from gods and muses to the personal. Sappho invented new styles and techniques, including what's known today as the sapphic meter, and she was one of the first to write her poetry in the first person, describing her own loves and losses and yearnings in a sensual and melodic style. Her phrasing is concise, direct, and picturesque. Like all poetry of the day, Sappho's was performed to the accompaniment of the lyre.

Attracted by her fame, maidens came from distant places to Sappho's finishing school to study poetry and music under her guidance. Her relationships with these young women were often intimate and intense, as can be seen in her fervent, astonishingly beautiful erotic poetry. Sappho became well known as a composer of wedding songs and wrote many for her beloved pupils when they married.

Out of nine complete volumes of poetry, only fragments and one complete composition, her "Hymn to Aphrodite," survive. The rest have been lost over the centuries—from neglect, from natural disasters, and from censorship of close-minded scholars. Possibly some of her works were burned in 1073 at Constantinople and Rome under Gregory VII.

Long after her death, Plato praised Sappho for her wisdom and charm; he called her the Tenth Muse. In the fifth century C.E., about a thousand years after Sappho lived, a statue of her was mounted in the gymnasium at Byzantium. Modern writers praise her as well. This enchanting woman remains an important cultural and literary figure, still studied these many centuries since her death. Not only is she important as a poet, but also as an example of a talented, self-directed, cultured woman dear to women seeking their voices and their muse.

56

Vercingetorix

Julius Caesar, emperor of Rome and all its empire, brilliant general and cruel invader, is a well-known historical figure, but far fewer people know of one of his greatest opponents: Vercingetorix. This idealistic young Celtic chieftain gave the old eagle, as Caesar was known, one of the most difficult conquests of his career.

In response to the invasions of the Roman army, many proud and independent Celtic tribes throughout Europe had been forming ever-shifting defensive alliances. The chieftain of one such tribe, the Arverni, was a high-spirited champion whom Caesar called Vercingetorix, meaning "over-king" (*ver-rix*) of warriors (*cingetos*), but whose Celtic name was probably Fearcuincedorigh, or "man who is chief of a hundred heads." As the Romans advanced into their lands, Vercingetorix ordered his people to burn crops and drive off the cattle so that Caesar's troops could not find provisions. Then the Celts ambushed the Roman supply convoys, hoping to starve the invading army in the snow-covered wilds of Gaul. The ambitious Caesar, however, marched his troops over the treacherous Alps in the dead of winter.

The hot-headed Celtic warriors engaged in many a battle with Caesar's organized, disciplined troops over the ensuing months, but eventually were forced to retreat. The final siege took place in the winter of 53 B.C.E., at Alesia (present-day Dijon). Alesia sat on a hill, with a three-mile-wide plain on one side and two rivers at its base, surrounded in the distance by high hills. Like other Celtic fortifications, Alesia was constructed of tree trunks laid side by side on the ground two feet apart, so that the depth of the wall was the length of the trees. These were crossed with beams laid crosswise, and the gaps were filled with earth and large stones, until the wall grew high. These walls resisted fire and battering ram.

Caesar moved his men into the valley and surrounded the fortress, intending to starve out the Celts gathered inside. The Roman general had his men work day after day building a series of concentric formations to protect his army from both the Celts in the fort and those who might attack from the outside. They dug broad ditches, some of which they filled with water; they built terraced ramparts up to nine feet high; and they mined the ground with all manner of spikes. The outer wall extended over thirteen miles in length and had twenty-three guard towers spaced around the perimeter.

During this time, the unruly Celts, dressed in their brightly colored checked *trews* (where the word "trousers" originated) and wielding swords and spears and yowling, made periodic sallies out of the fort to harry the laborers. Meanwhile, before the enclosing walls and trenches closed them off entirely, Vercingetorix sent horsemen under cover of darkness back to their own tribes to make alliances and seek reinforcements.

Caesar's troops, their defenses completed, attacked the fort. As the siege continued and food ran low, the desperate Celts turned out their women, children, and the aged to surrender to the Romans, in hopes that the Romans would feed them, knowing that slavery was their future. Caesar refused to encumber his army with the burden of women and children. For days the refugees stayed trapped, begging refuge. They died, cold and starving, on the plains between the ramparts, as both Romans and Celts looked on. In spite of the valor shown by the Celts in this desperate situation, the shameful way they treated the women and children stains their memory.

The Celts eventually saw the futility of their circumstances. Vercingetorix offered himself to Caesar to save his remaining companions. According to Caesar's written account, Vercingetorix said, "I did not undertake the war for private ends, but in the cause of national liberty. And since I must now accept my fate, I place myself at your disposal. Make amends to the Romans by killing me or surrender me alive as you think best." Writing a hundred years later, the Greek historian Plutarch claims that Vercingetorix surrendered with dramatic dignity: wearing his most colorful armor and riding his carefully groomed horse, the

Celt rode a circle around Caesar, dismounted, removed his armor, and placed it at Caesar's feet in surrender.

Vercingetorix was taken prisoner to Rome and held captive for six years. When in July 45 B.C.E. Julius Caesar staged a grand, triumphal procession to celebrate his many victories, Vercingetorix was among the trophies he displayed. Like the captives from other conquered peoples, Vercingetorix was dressed in native garb and full armor, but chained at hands and feet, in subjugation and humiliation. After this glorious public display, Caesar had Vercingetorix led to a prison cell and either stabbed or strangled to death.

Because of his ability to organize highly individualistic compatriots and to strategize against a well-supported, disciplined fighting force, together with his courage in resisting the mighty Caesar and his pursuit of empire, the little-known Pagan warrior Vercingetorix inspires pride in the heart of many.

IV

SCIENCE AND TECHNOLOGY

When we look at our heritage, we can see thousands of ways in which human culture has benefited from sciences and technologies discovered, explored, and invented by our Pagan ancestors. The science of mathematics informed the development of architecture. The science of astronomy lead to the technology of calendars and time keeping, the timing of sowing and harvesting crops. Tools such as the spear, bow and arrows, plow, and mortar and pestle precipitated great leaps of cultural development whenever and wherever they were invented. Technologies such as agriculture, milling, tanning, smithcraft, and boat building allowed for the expansion of human habitation. Canal building and irrigation expanded the ability to provide excess food. The sacred technologies of brewing, baking, food preservation, pottery, and weaving fur-

ther enhanced human life. The pharmacist's trade is indicated by a mortar and pestle, tools with which she grinds and blends magical healing substances. Brewers have barrels crafted by coopers. The smithy signals his trade with a horseshoe. Let's look at some of these contributions together.

57

Baking and Ovens

The grasses growing from Mother Earth—wheat, oats, barley, rye, and other grains—have nourished people since the Stone Age. Evidence shows that our ancestors ate solid cakes made from stone-crushed barley and wheat. Both have been found in ruins dating from 10,000 B.C.E. in present-day Jordan, and circa 7500 B.C.E., in the ancient city of Catal Hoyuk in western Turkey. Using dried whole or cracked grains mixed with water, our ancestors cooked porridges. They also made flat cakes baked directly on coals or hot stones, like our present-day crepes, pita, rice cakes, papadum, nan, and pancakes.

In order to break the wheat down into a more refined and digestible flour, grain was originally ground between two stones or with mortar and pestle. Ancient grinding holes for grinding grains and even nuts are found worldwide. Instead of using person power or oxen or donkeys, around 100 B.C.E. Romans began to use waterpower for milling flour, leading to the establishment of mills.

Women traditionally performed the magical process of transforming grasses and seeds into life-sustaining bread. The sacred technologies of food preservation and the arts of brewing and baking are women's arts. Beginning at the harvest, women bound the cut bundles of wheat into sheaves. These were laid in rows and flailed by the women to beat the grain from the heads. Then women winnowed the seed to allow the chaff to blow out. Sieves made of woven grass came into use around 6,000 B.C.E. After this, they ground the flour. Their grinding was a rhythmic, time-consuming, labor-intensive act, performed in community, accompanied by song or prayer, that invited trancing and the telling of stories.

The first true breads were baked in the Mediterranean and Middle East around 2500 B.C.E. when fermented doughs were added. A leavening agent called "barm" caused a loaf to raise and fill with air bubbles, producing a lighter bread. Before there were ovens, bread was baked under a heated clay dome. Assyrian bakers placed the doughs in heated earthen pots, sealed them, and buried them in the ground to bake. Greeks developed front-loading bread ovens as well as a wide variety of doughs and styles of serving bread with other food. They made loaves in symbolic shapes, such as crescent mooncakes and round suncakes, like today's hot cross buns.

Bakeries have been found in the ruins of Pompeii. Roman bakers made rich breads by adding milk, eggs, butter, and cheese, oyster bread to be eaten with oysters, and *speusticus*, or "hurry bread," for the person on the go. Bakers formed the Roman Bakers' Guild, called *Collegium Pistorum*, in 168 B.C.E. Ceres (source of our word "cereal"), goddess of grain, presided over their work. Bakers from different cities competed in bread baking, with the victor being crowned with a laurel wreath. The best bakers were said to come from Phoenicia, Lydia, and Cappadocia. Bakers served a seven-year apprenticeship, after which they and their families enjoyed special status in Roman society. Neither bakers nor their families were permitted to mix with "comedians and gladiators" and they were forbidden from attending performances in the amphitheater, probably to keep them from being exposed to disease. Bakers were the only craftspeople who were freemen of the city; all other trades were performed by slaves. Over the years of human history bread has been so important as a principal foodstuff, and the farmers who grew the grain, the millers who ground it, and the bakers who made it so important to survival, that bread riots have sparked revolutions and social upheavals.

On Lughnasad, or Lammas ("loaf mass"), Witches in my home community place loaves wrapped in foil in the belly of our wicker man. We celebrate the death of the Sun god and the gifts of the grain of the field when we dance around the burning man. When the fire has consumed him and his spirit and our spells have been released, we share the magic of the sweet hot body of the god. Other Pagans celebrate the spirit of the grain as the John Barleycorn, who personifies the spirit of the kernel when he is sown in spring, ripens in summer, is cut down in autumn, and feeds us through the winter; he also provides hearty beverage for us to wash him down. Like the ancient Greeks, Scandinavians, and bakers around the world, NeoPagans bake mooncakes, cakes shaped like animals, people, or objects, for our celebrations. I'm happy to see these ancient sacred arts being pursued by NeoPagans of all genders, using the energy from their hands and hearts to create food for each other.

See **Agriculture, Brewing, Pottery, Demeter and Persephone/Kore**

58

Brewing

Brewing is the alchemical art and science of making a beverage by boiling, steeping, or mixing various ingredients together in water. Beer and mead, an alcoholic drink made from honey ("from the meadow"), are likely the oldest manufactured drinks and survive today as two of the most magical of beverages. Beer making is an ancient sacred technology of food preservation. A vase unearthed in modern-day Iran contains traces of beer from more than five thousand years ago, and evidence of beer making was found at Catal Hoyuk, a city in Anatolia that was occupied from about 6250 to 5400 B.C.E.

Briefly, beer is made by slightly heating grain to force it to begin sprouting, a process called malting. This activates sugars within the grain. Water is then dripped over the malted grain and a tea of sorts—

called the wort—is created. The wort is boiled and flavoring, most often hops, is added. The mixture is cooled and yeast is added. The yeast consumes the sugar and produces alcohol in a process called fermentation. When fermentation is complete the product is siphoned into containers and chilled. This is beer. The Celtic goddess Bridget's gift, mead, is brewed according to the same basic recipe with honey replacing grain as the sugar. Flavorings are sometimes added to the wort to produce mead variants: adding fruit changes the flavor profile of the drink to form a melomel, while adding spices creates metheglin (spiced mead). Honey is sacred to many deities and in many cultures.

Beer came before wine everywhere in the ancient world; the celebratory orgies of Thrace, Phrygia, the Feast of Tabernacles, and others all used beer for its intoxicating ritual powers. Some experts believe Dionysus became associated with wine only after appearing as Sabazios, the god of beer. The sacredness our Pagan ancestors attributed to the art of brewing is attested by hymns to Ninkasi, the Sumerian goddess of brewing, composed more than four thousand years ago. Egypt produced hundreds of thousands of gallons of beer every year, and the Romans had special priests to prepare the brews for religious celebrations. The Pagan association with brewing and Earth's bounty were maintained in symbol: the English folksong "John Barleycorn" is but one ode to beer found in music.

Wine is made in a similar way, though we typically don't think of wine as a brewed drink. Grapes naturally contain the correct balance of sugars and other ingredients, though wine can be made from any nontoxic plant material. NeoPagans today make May Wine, for example, by steeping woodruff in a bottle of white wine for up to a week. Woodruff is used probably because its small white flowers bloom in May. It also may have been used, along with hawthorn and other flowering plants, in the "Bringing in the May" rituals of the British Isles. Wassail, a popular Yule drink, is often red wine heated and mulled with spices.

Brewing is inherently magickal and highly versatile and has seen a resurgence in the NeoPagan community. Making beer, mead, and other brews is easy, adaptable, and safe. (Unlike distilling beverages—vaporizing, then cooling and collecting the condensed liquid—the worst that can happen with a bad batch of beer is a horrible smell and a bad taste.) Mead and other honeyed drinks (including modern-day Irish crèmes and some Irish whiskeys) are effective tools in Celtic-oriented worship. The brew is easily manipulated to produce the desired ritual effect. Altering the ingredients and the alcohol content by adding a special fruit for flavoring or additional sugar/malt for higher alcohol levels to reflect the preferences of deity and practitioner alike is simple because the basic production process is the same. For instance, Brigit prefers a pure mead or perhaps a beer with oats in it. Other deities may well prefer raspberry-, strawberry-, or blackberry-flavored mead or beer. Mediterranean Dionysus prefers a more highly intoxicating brew than, say, the continental stag god Cernunnos.

See **Baking, Bridget, Dionysus, May Day.**

59

Calendars

From the beginning of human existence people have kept track of days and night, moons and years. Early human beings carved or scratched marks on wood or rock to mark the passage of time. Women, and possibly men as well, undoubtedly took note of the synchronicity of women's bleeding times with the cycle of the moon. There is widespread evidence dating back to the Paleolithic Age of such counting of days and nights and moons. People could predict the seasons for hunting, and later planting, animal husbandry, and navigation, by observing that approximately thirteen lunations (moon cycles) occurred between one spring and the next. Human beings also learned to predict meteorological phenomena such as the annual flooding of river valleys like the Nile in Egypt, dry seasons and monsoons, and seasonal winds such as the sirocco and trade winds.

As they accumulated observations and communicated about them, people devised calendars. Calendars evolved in the ancient Near East and Mediterranean world, and independently in Central America, where people calculated complex calendars based on celestial constellations from 1000 B.C.E. The invention of calendars, just like the invention of clocks, made for more efficiency in the growing complexity of early cultures. Calendars assigned days and dates, small sequences of days into weeks, and larger sequences of days into months, months into semesters, quarters, and years.

The concept of a seven-day week arose in the ancient Middle East and spread throughout the world through commerce. Beginning with the Babylonians, the seven-day week was adopted by Jews and was later carried throughout the Mediterranean and beyond by the expanding Roman Empire. English names use today for the days of the week are Pagan. Each day in a week of seven days corresponds to one of the seven celestial bodies visible to the naked eye. Each day is named for a deity; the English names today come mainly from Saxon gods. Sunday is named for Sunna, the Scandinavian sun goddess, or Sunne, the Saxon sun god. Monday is the moon's day. Tuesday is the Germanic god of war and justice Tyr's day, associated with the planet Mars. Wednesday is called by the name of Wodan or Odin, also Mercury, the quick-witted travelers' god; Thursday is Thor's, bringer of thunder, associated with Jupiter. Friday is sacred to Freya or Freyr, to the planet Venus, the morning and the evening star. Because it is the day sacred to Venus, Friday is the best day to do a love spell. Saturday is Saturn's day.

Just as with the names of the days, the months in the Gregorian calendar used today retain their Pagan names. For example, our secular New Year begins with the month of January, named for Janus, the two-faced Roman god who looks backward and foreword, who presides at doors and gates; February is named for the Roman god of purification, Februus.

Today there are not only lunar and solar calendars, but also agricultural, meteorological, tidal, siderial, and many other ways of calculating time. We've come a long way from the primitive calendars made by our Pagan ancestors to the complex calendars of the twenty-first century C.E.

See **Stonehenge, Carnac.**

60

Clocks

As far back as six thousand years ago the peoples of the Middle East and North Africa constructed clocks, as distinct from calendars, although some of their methods entailed the tracking of celestial bodies just as calendars do. As cultures grew more complex, with their attendant bureaucracies and religions, the efficient organization of time became desirable.

Whatever the Sumerians knew of clock making has been lost in the mists of the past, but history does reveal that the Egyptians formally divided their days into something similar to the hours we know today. They began keeping daily time with obelisks as early as 3500 B.C.E. These are tall, slender, tapering four-sided structures made of rock and can form a kind of sundial. When the sun is directly overhead at noon, the obelisk casts little to no shadow; markings around the base indicate further subdivisions of time into hours and portions thereof. Obelisks also showed the longest and shortest days of the year by the length of the shadow. The Egyptians divided the day into morning and afternoon, ante meridian and post meridian (a.m. and p.m.), just as we designate them to this day. Around 1500 B.C.E., Egyptians invented another type of shadow clock, to measure the passage of hours, the kind we know as the sundial. The shadow cast by the sundial's pointer indicated the hour. This was probably the first portable clock. Sundials and obelisks, however, didn't help determine time during the night. Beginning around 300 B.C.E., the *hemicycle*, which looked like a half-bowl cut into the edge of a squared block, served as another form of sundial. Thirteen different types of sundials were in used in Asia Minor, Greece, and Italy by the year 30 B.C.E.

Around 600 B.C.E., Egyptians devised the *merkhet* from the vertically aligned central rib of a palm frond. Two merkhets were aligned with the Pole Star to establish a north-south orientation. This permitted the counting of nighttime hours by observing when certain other stars crossed the meridian.

Another type of clock, the water clock, did not depend on the observation of celestial bodies, but rather on the time it took for drops of water to be emptied from a container via a small hole. The Greeks called these clocks *clepsydras* (water thief) when they began using them about 325 B.C.E. Clepsydras were stone vessels containing markings on the inside to measure the hours. Either bowl-shaped or cylindrical in form, and occasionally made of metal, clepsydras held water that dripped from a small hole at a nearly constant rate. The oldest water clock, dating from 1500 B.C.E., was found in the tomb of Pharaoh Amenhotep I of Egypt. Clepsydras were used in third-century C.E. China as well. Greek and Roman astronomers and horologists, during the centuries between 100 B.C.E. and 500 C.E., constructed elaborate mechanized water clocks. Some even moved pointers, dials, and astrological models of the universe (as it was understood then), some rang bells or gongs tolling the time, and some opened doors and windows to show little figures of people, like today's Alpine cuckoo clocks.

Other early ways of measuring time were oil lamps with marked reservoirs, candles marked in increments, and sand glasses, which we recognize today as hourglasses.

In the first century B.C.E. the Greek astronomer Andronikos oversaw the construction of an octagonal structure called the Tower of the Winds. This clock showed the seasons of the year and astrological dates as well as the hours.

The invention of clocks by our Pagan ancestors has contributed to the advancement of culture. However, in postmodern society we have a tendency to be ruled by clocks. We see clocks in most public places, we wear portable clocks, we schedule our days rigidly. Much as I appreciate clocks, I think we are better served by abandoning them now and then. In fact, visible timepieces interfere with the work done in magic circles, when we are in sacred space, "between the worlds and beyond time."

See **Writing.**

61

Hanging Gardens of Babylon

Nebuchadnezzar II (604–562 B.C.E.) ruled Babylon at the height of its glory. During his reign, he built many new temples, a palace, defensive walls with 250 watchtowers, and 100 bronze gates (including one dedicated to the goddess Ishtar), and he paved processional ways. The ancient city was also site of the temple known as the Tower of Babel, dedicated to the double-headed Babylonian god of magic and incantations Marduk.

Nebuchadnezzar allied his kingdom with the neighboring dynasty of Media by marrying the daughter of the Median king. This woman, Amyritis, grew depressed in the flat, sun-baked desert of Babylon and homesick for the lush green mountains where she grew up. So, it is said, Nebuchadnezzar created the gardens to cheer her up, the famed Hanging Gardens of Babylon. In the ancient world the gardens stood as one of the most spectacular testimonies to love, engineering, empire, and hubris. Although they are also a testimony to self-glorification, the gardens demonstrate a sophisticated knowledge of hydraulics and an architectural role model unsurpassed. The lush gardens created a splendid artificial mountain rising from the hot desert near the banks of the Euphrates River in the ancient city of Babylon, in Iraq, an area today racked by discord.

The gardens were comprised of a series of terraces rising from seventy-five to three hundred feet high, with stairways leading to the uppermost terraces. They were supported by an intricate structure of stone pillars, brick walls, and palm tree trunk beams. Stone was not a local resource. Imported stone is known to have been used in only two places in Babylon: the citadel and the garden. Clever architects made the palm trunks watertight to protect them from the irrigation water drawn from the nearby river by covering them with mats of reed and bitumen, with two layers of baked mud brick on top of that, and then a final layer of lead. The bricks, too, were covered so that the drenched earth of the gardens above wouldn't rot the foundation.

There were fourteen vaulted rooms and underground crypts. An elaborate tunnel and pulley system brought groundwater to the top terrace. The energy to power the chain pump came from slaves who cranked two large wheels, one at the top and one at the bottom. Buckets hanging from the chain were continuously dipped into the Euphrates. At the top, the buckets tipped and dumped water into an upper pool. Water could then be released by gates into channels that acted as artificial streams to water the gardens.

The Greek geographer Strabo, writing in the first century B.C.E., describes the garden as having hollow cube-shaped pillars filled with earth to allow large trees to grow.

The completed gardens had fountains, pools, and artificial waterfalls to create humidity. Fruits, flowers, and exotic animals lived in the cool shade of trees. A contemporary description says that the gardens contained "cedar, cypress, myrtle, juniper, almond, date palm, ebony, olive, oak, terebinth, nuts, ash, firs, nightshade, willow, pomegranate, plum, pear, quince, fig, and grapevine."

The gardens lasted until the time of Alexander the Great in the fourth century B.C.E. Scholars had disputed the existence of these fabulous gardens. However, in 1899 a German archaeologist named Robert

Koldewey found convincing evidence. His excavations of Babylon turned up fourteen large rooms with stone arch ceilings, as well as another room with three large holes that could have been the location of the chain pumps that watered the garden from the roof down.

Today we can but wonder at the ingenuity, technology, and cooperation, not to mention religious dedication, that resulted in the construction of such a wonder. We are reminded of the magical quality of gardens to offer solace, perspective, and serenity, to help to reconnect us with growing things, to show us comfort amid their sacred beauty.

See **Seven Wonders of the Ancient World.**

62

Leather and Tanning

We know that our prehistoric ancestors clothed themselves in the hides and furs of wild animals. To prevent decay, they cured pelts with grease and smoke. They used them mainly for tents, containers, coverings, garments, and shoes. In addition to being an important material for making clothing, leather, together with wood, formed the basis of much ancient technology. Colored leather, sandals, bags, and clothing were found in tombs in Nubia as far back as 5000 B.C.E. Egyptian tomb paintings from 3000 B.C.E. show tanners at work. Skins were also used to make parchment and vellum for writing. The earliest known document written on leather is an Egyptian scroll dating from 2000 B.C.E.

The process of tanning stinks—it literally is smelly. Important as tanning was to early cultures, the work was done by the poor, who were relegated to the outskirts of town to keep noxious odors away from the main populace. Tanners made leather from goatskin, sheepskin, pigskin, and cow hide. Other animal skins used for leather throughout the world include snakes, crocodiles, ostriches, emus, and stingrays. People made such valuable items as waterskins, bags, harnesses, boats, sails, sandals, boots, armor, quivers, and scabbards from leather—and many kinds of skins were used for drumheads. Sumerians used copper studs to affix leather to chariot wheels around 2500 B.C.E.

European tanners used fats, minerals such as alum, the bark of oak and hemlock, gallnuts, sumac leaves, and the wood, nuts, and leaves of the chestnut tree in the tanning processes. The fats imparted pliability and made the leather tougher. Native Americans of North America used animal fat, livers, and brains to produce chamois. Chamoising involves treating the hides with fats, hanging it to dry, then napping it on both sides with emery or another abrasive to create a soft, absorbent finish.

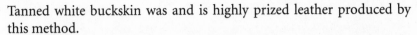

Tanned white buckskin was and is highly prized leather produced by this method.

Its qualities of flexibility, thickness, toughness, and durability make leather far superior to cloth for many uses, and it remains an important material for shoes, belts of all kinds, clothing, pouches and bags, protection, and for many other common objects. Whatever gods oversaw the work in the tanneries have been lost to time, and despite the unpleasantness of the process and the fact that the work was done by people on the fringes of society, undoubtedly the work was considered sacred. Furthermore, our Pagan ancestors wasted nothing. Tanners put leftover scraps of hide into vats of water for months, then boiled off the water to produce glue. Modern consumer culture would do well to look to these ancestors. They provide us with righteous role models for economy of consumption, for careful use of natural resources that resulted in little to no waste.

See **Papyrus, Parchment/Vellum, and Paper.**

63

Linen

Linen is cloth woven from the fibers of a blue-flowered herbaceous plant called flax. Before the invention of linen, our earliest Pagan ancestors, those who hunted game in the forests and savannahs, those who gathered nuts, berries, roots, and leaves, clothed themselves in the skins of the animals they had killed and eaten. Later herding peoples learned to sheer, card, spin, and weave wool from their flocks of sheep and goats. They began to dress in woolen garments. Eventually, with the cultivation of plants, agricultural peoples learned to use plant fibers to create thread to weave into cloth for clothing and other uses. This is linen. The oldest linen fragments, in all stages of manufacture (straw, seed and seed capsules, fibers, yarns, ropes, and fabrics) were found in Stone Age (8000 B.C.E.) lake dwellings in what is now Switzerland. Linen came into use in the civilizations of the river valleys of the Tigris and Euphrates and the blue Nile five to eight thousand years ago. Called *shenu* in Egyptian, *linon* in Greek, and *linum* in Latin, linen was cultivated from the flax plant *linum usitatissimum*, or "most useful linen."

Enterprising Phoenician traders brought flax seeds, and the knowledge of growing it and making linen, from the Mediterranean to Gaul, the Lowlands, the British Islands, and Hibernia, so when the Romans conquered Gaul and Belgium in 56 B.C.E., they were surprised to find beautiful fields of flax and fine linens made in this region. Linen cultivation spread even farther with the expansion of the Roman Empire. The Irish embraced linen work and developed it into a fine art.

Linen manufacture is labor intensive, requiring the work of many over a period of months or longer. Women did much of this sacred work. They wove and stitched their magic into each piece of cloth they worked. It is women's work to birth the children and to midwife birth. Women swaddled their infants in pure white linen at birth. And at the end of life, women did the holy work of washing the dead and wrapping them in linen winding-sheets.

Fine linens have been found in Egyptian tombs dating to 6000 B.C.E. The mummy wrappings of Pharaoh Rameses II, who died in 1258 B.C.E., were found in a perfect state of preservation when his tomb was opened in 1861 C.E. Likewise, the mummy of the daughter of a priest of Ammon who died 2500 years ago is wrapped in perfectly preserved linen. When the tomb of Tutankhamen was opened, only its linen curtains had remained intact while all other fabrics had long since disintegrated into dust.

The more linen is washed, the softer and more luminous it becomes. Linen's remarkable strength, luster, and durability made it a desirable fabric for royal robes and sacerdotal vestments from earliest times. In ancient Egypt, Israel, and throughout the Mediterranean cultures, linen was fabric made into the curtains around sacred shrines. It was used for altar cloths, just as it is used today. Plutarch wrote that the priests of Isis wore linen because of its purity. Ecclesiastics wore linen robes and head wrappings. Garments of pure white linen symbolize the purity of the virgin bride. Linen dressings were used to cure skin diseases, including leprosy. Linens have always been used to bandage wounds and keep them clean and free of infection. Linen has other interesting uses. For instance, the first condom was a linen sheath used by Egyptians around 1000 B.C.E. as a prophylactic against disease; from linen we make paper and linen provides the artists' canvas; and linseed oil is used in inks, paints, and soap.

The loose white undergarment worn throughout the lands of Celtic speakers for centuries is called a *linye*. It has giant sleeves that serve as pocket and purse. NeoPagans wear Irish linyes, Roman togas, Greek chitons, and other linen garments. We remember and honor our Pagan heritage when we continue to spread luxurious linen on our sacred altars.

64

Navigation

Navigation, from the Latin *navis*, ship, and *agere*, to drive, came from two distinct sources in our Pagan past. Polynesians performed the amazing, to our modern eyes, feat of crossing thousands of miles of open ocean in canoes and other small vessels. With no instruments, only their memory and intelligence, these early sailors traveled from tiny island to tiny island throughout Polynesia and the South Pacific.

Polynesian navigators enjoyed very high status in their societies due to their skills and importance to their people. Each island had its own guild of navigators who maintained strict secrecy about their methods of navigating and building boats. They memorized the positions of the stars, seasonal weather patterns, and unusual weather phenomena. Polynesian navigators were able to plan their travel according to times of the day and year and which wildlife congregated in particular positions. They even observed and understood the directions of swells and the colors of the sea.

Originally, navigators in the West used only dead reckoning, estimating their position by the navigator's experience of tides, currents, and winds.

Early Mediterranean sailors observed the relative positions of the sun, the moon, and other celestial bodies to assist their movement through the waters. Most were able to find Polaris, the North Star, in order to orient themselves. By using a dual sundial called a diptych in combination with a plumb bob, they could also determine latitude. Two other early navigation tools used by ancient Bronze Age Cretan sailors were the hourglass and the compass rose. Helmsmen or young boys were responsible for turning the hourglasses. The compass rose was a painted panel of wood placed in front of the helmsman. It was oriented with the pole star or diptych. Of course, none of these methods could be used in fog or the dark of night.

The Mediterranean navigator's diary, called a rutter, proved to be his most important instrument, which allowed for the development of great trade routes that spread commerce throughout the Mediterranean and as far as the south coast of Britain. The rutter in the West served a similar function to that of the Polynesian navigators' guilds in that its secrets enabled them to travel with increasingly reliable knowledge and skills. For the people of Polynesia, their navigators could be relied upon to take them safely to another island when food grew scarce on one.

Navigation grew more sophisticated after the invention of the magnetic compass in China around 300 C.E. With this instrument, which relied on the magnetic pull of the north, sailors could navigate at night and in foggy weather. A hundred years later advanced metallurgy led to the construction of astrolabes (from *astro,* star, and *labe,* to take), which enabled sailors to take a reading from the star's position and determine where they were.

Sailors dedicated their ships and themselves to deities of travel and commerce, such as Hermes, and they came to know intimately the powers and moods of the many gods (Poseidon, Manannan), goddesses (Tiamat, Mari), sea nymphs, whirlpools, rocks, and winds they encountered in their travels. They sought their divine protection, made offerings in propitiation, and appealed to them when they needed divine help, such as a good wind.

Today we have not only buoys and lighthouses, but also radio and satellite navigation, but for most of human existence people relied on navigational techniques developed by Pagans to travel to all parts of Earth.

See **Clocks.**

65

Papyrus, Parchment/Vellum, and Paper

Thanks to ancient Egyptians and their neighbors in Palestine, Syria, and southern Europe we have papyrus on which to write. Around 2400 B.C.E. or earlier people in these regions learned to moisten strips of the thin pith of the sedge Cyperus plant and lay them next to each other on a board. Another layer of pith was then added perpendicularly to the first and the two were pressed together. They beat this with hammers, which ruptured the plant tissues thus releasing the sap. This process glued the strips together, after which they were dried in the sun. Rubbing the papyrus with flat stones until it polished smooth, many sheets of papyrus were joined and rolled on wood rods to make scrolls.

At about the same time (or, some sources say, as early as 1500 B.C.E.) people in the Middle East began making parchment from animal skins. The earliest reference to the term "parchment" appears in 30 C.E. The process of making parchment—made from calf, goat, gazelles, the animal depending upon geographic location—differs from tanning primarily in that the wet pelts are dried under tension. This changes the natural fiber weave of the skin to a horizontal-layered structure. By the second century B.C.E., the technology had improved and hair was removed from the skins; they were scraped, polished, stretched, and finally rubbed with chalk and pumice.

Mature animals have tougher skin; skin from the belly area is smoother and looser. Vellum (related to the word "veal") is a finer grade of parchment made from the skin of young or, sometimes, unborn calves or lambs. Vellum tends to be whiter and more pliable than parchment.

Early texts were written on parchment in gold and silver inks, often tinted purple to set off inks. Amusingly, after the invention of parchment the Greeks and Romans still wrote on wax, for they considered parchment barbaric.

Thanks belong to an official in the royal Chinese court, Ts'ai Lun, who invented paper making in 105 B.C.E. People previously wrote on pure silk—in fact, the Chinese ideogram for paper means "silk"—but the proliferation of literature and the development of the animal hair-brush and calligraphy called for something more practical and less expensive to write on.

Around 700 C.E., the Arabs won a battle with the Chinese in the central Asian city of Samarkand. Two of the captured Chinese were paper makers; they were able to gain their freedom in exchange for teaching the Arabs the technology of making paper. Arabs improved paper when they began using the more durable linen.

In Europe, paper was made primarily from flax and hemp, which was shredded and soaked in water to produce a pulp. The pulp fibers were then meshed and matted into sheets, dried, and pressed. In fact, early paper was called "cloth parchment." Paper making has changed many times over the years due to economic growth, historical influences, the availability of raw materials/resources, and social issues.

In the United States, paper was made from recycled linen and cotton rags. Trees weren't used for paper until the 1850s, when there was a seemingly endless supply of virgin timber for the taking, and a government bent on expansion from coast to coast subsidized the paper-making industry. The government gave tax credit for resource depletion and lower freight rates. In today's world, with the dwindling supply of natural resources, this seems outrageous.

The Pagan invention of paper led to books, and the availability of books led to schools and universities, as well as a general increase in literacy. Previously only nobility and upper classes had the leisure to learn to read and write. The change from oral culture to a written one also changed our thinking process. We no longer had to memorize and carry all knowledge in our head. Visual arts, too, were changed, as paper provided artists with a cheap medium on which to sketch out their designs before committing them to canvas or fresco walls. This in turn led to the new art form of sketching. Paper making led to expansion of business and eventually to the development of the modern corporation. These blessings are mixed, to be sure, but we can look to our Pagan ancestors for answers. They used every part of the animals they killed. They knew no such thing as landfill, wasted nothing, and recycled anything that could be recycled.

See **Libraries and Books, Writing, Leather and Tanning.**

66

Pompeii and Herculaneum

In the course of two days in late August 79 C.E., two ancient Italian cities, Pompeii and Herculaneum, were destroyed during the eruption of Mount Vesuvius. Both cities were founded by Pagan peoples centuries earlier, although they were quite different from each other.

Pompeii, built on a bed of prehistoric lava, coalesced as a city in the seventh century B.C.E., making it about eight hundred years old when it vanished. Its founders were Etruscan, a civilization in present-day Italy that preceded the Roman Empire. Of course, since the Greeks traveled and traded widely throughout the Mediterranean region and beyond, their influence was strong in Pompeii. Excavations have revealed a terrace with Doric columns (from the Dorian Greeks) built in the sixth century. An elaborate system of aqueducts and lead-pipe plumbing supplied the houses with running water and allowed for luxurious public baths, with heated water and marble linings.

The remains left after the volcano's eruption reveal that Pompeii at the time of its demise was a place bustling with activity. The amphitheater, forum full of stall keepers, taverns, bakeries, brothels, and the graffiti-covered walls—all show what a busy place the city was in its last days. The forum contained innumerable statues, probably of both deities and dignitaries. There were several temples, including one dedicated to Apollo, one to the goddess Fortuna Augusta, and another to both Vespasian, the emperor of Rome who died a few months before the eruption, and Jupiter, the patriarch of the Roman pantheon; it was common to dedicate temples to both the emperor and gods at the time.

One of the more elegant streets in Pompeii was the Via di Mercurio, named for the god of streets and travelers, Mercury. The House of Venus is dedicated to the goddess of love. The Pompeiians enjoyed the pleasures of the flesh: many frescoes depict various acts of lovemaking. In fact, the most famous images found show the god Priapus with a phallus so huge one wonders how he could walk.

Perhaps the most beautiful of the city's buildings was the Villa dei Misteri, or Villa of the Mysteries, where fifty-five rooms, many painted predominantly in the color later called Pompeii red, are adorned with images inspired by the Dionysian mysteries celebrated there.

Herculaneum was a younger city than Pompeii, having been founded in the fourth century B.C.E. With about four or five thousand inhabitants, Herculaneum was also smaller in area and in population. It was also the more peaceful, its lush greenery, vineyards, and refined architecture attracting vacationers from the Roman aristocracy. Overall, Herculaneum was the more subdued of the two cities, something like the difference between coastal resort towns that have gambling and those that don't.

The remains of people, animals, plants, buildings, artifacts, and artwork found in these two sophisticated cities, caught as they were in midlife, provide a unique snapshot of the life of our Pagan ancestors.

See **Aphrodite, Dionysus, Mercury/Hermes, Cerne Abbas Giant.**

67

Pottery

Archaeologists think that the earliest pottery may have been used for religious or magical ceremonies around 10,000 B.C.E., although it's clear that women also used pottery in domestic rituals as well as for decorative display. The earliest pottery vessels in the world have been found in southwestern Japan, in fact. They were made fourteen to sixteen thousand years ago and were undecorated. By ten thousand years ago, ceramics were manufactured throughout China. Then, five thousand years ago pottery was found in virtually all river-based early civilizations throughout the world, including in the Americas, and all of it seems to have been developed independently. The earliest was often coiled and left to dry in the sun. Later people discovered that baking made clay items stronger.

Women have always had a special relationship with fired clay. They made clay vessels for cooking, for carrying, storing, and serving foods, and for holding water twelve to thirteen thousand years ago. Pottery offers some of the earliest evidence of how our Pagan ancestors lived; some even retain handprints. The invention of pottery radically transformed society: it improved the storage of grains and liquids by better preserving them. Pottery also increased the ways in which food could be prepared.

Clay was plentiful on the banks of the Tigris and Euphrates where we find much ancient pottery. In addition to making clay vessels, early Sumerians made beads, built temples, and kept records and accounts on clay. Crude Neolithic pottery—jars and bowls with painted or incised designs in triangle and zigzag patterns; figurines of women with exaggerated hips and obvious breasts—has been found in Israel and Lebanon. Jericho engaged in trade in turquoise, salt, sulfur, asphalt, shells, and greenstone axes. By 4000 B.C.E. Egyptian potters crafted pottery with more refined shapes and decoration, adding ornamentations, patterns, lines, and decorative borders; colored pottery appeared about the same time. Egyptians and Phoenicians made great and small images in pottery—of gods, men, and animals. Two thousand years later, also in Egypt, the potter's wheel was invented. Glazing was introduced at the same time, and fired bricks and tiles followed soon thereafter.

The oldest pottery in North America, made during the Early Woodland period (three thousand to twenty-two hundred years ago), was found in Illinois. Prior to then, containers had been made of wood, plant fiber, or leather. The makers of this early American pottery used a mixture of clay, temper (stone, sand, shell added to strengthen and ensure even drying), and water, to which they applied abstract symbols.

The best-known ancient Pagan pottery, however, comes from the golden age of Grecian civilization. The Greeks introduced new shapes, forms, and uses. They added painting and other coloration, molded reliefs, and ornamental fluting. They made vases in the forms of animals, birds, and human heads. The Greeks also made clay bricks and tiles that they used in their buildings. The best Greek pottery used two colors—black and red. There are four classifications of subjects on Greek pottery. One is images relating to mythology; another relates to the Heroic Age and traditions of early Greek history; a third depicts images from known history; and a fourth shows contemporary manners and customs.

The largest pottery object was the *pithos*, which was also by Egyptians and Romans. Pithos were used as cellars for the storage and preservation of provisions, and, like Oscar the Grouch's home in a garbage can, the pithos sometimes served as a refuge of the poor who might be seeking shelter.

The most common form of vase was an *amphora*, also used by Egyptians and Phoenicians. The amphora had a long, cylindrical or ovoid body originally with pointed base to be pressed into sand or soil, and two handles. Amphorae ranged in size from a small two- or three-inch drug vase to those large enough to hold oil, grain, fruit, wine, or water. Unglazed amphorae were commonly used for preserving and transporting wines, oils, and fruit throughout the Eastern world. They often had their makers' names stamped on handles, and sometimes a name of a magistrate.

The *krater* was a gigantic punch bowl. Wine was dipped out in the *oinochoe*, or wine pitcher, and poured into cups for guests. The *kylix* was a broad, shallow cup with handles. Another form of drinking cup was the *rhyton*, made in many odd shapes so that it could not be set down until it was empty. The finest wines then known were poured into the kylixes and rhytons of the guests by young pages.

When the practice of cremating the dead became the custom, their ashes were kept in beautiful vases. Vases were among the prizes given to the victors in the Olympic games, and when the athlete died, his ashes were kept in the vase that had been his prize.

We can imagine the splendor of a Greek banquet and the honored place of the funeral urn.

68

Seven Wonders of the Ancient World

The Seven Wonders of the Ancient World—a phrase filled with romance, but how many can name these wonders? All but one are lost to time. Two are tombs. All have Pagan religious significance and four are dedicated to specific deities. The list of the Seven Wonders was actually compiled around the second century B.C.E. Callimachus of Cyrene, chief librarian at the Alexandria Mouseion, supposedly wrote about them, but his work was destroyed when the library was put to the torch by Caesar's forces in 48 B.C.E.

The oldest and only surviving wonder is the *Great Pyramid of Giza*, built during the Fourth Dynasty (2608–2544 B.C.E.) in Memphis, today part of greater Cairo.

The fabled *Hanging Gardens of Babylon* were built by Nebuchadnezzar II (604–52 B.C.E.) in Babylon. This structure is so spectacular, complex, and unusual that it's described more fully in another entry.

In the mid-fifth century B.C.E., Greeks erected a forty-foot statue of their father god *Zeus*, in the Temple of Zeus at Olympia, site of the Olympic Games. Sculpted by Phidias, the same man who sculpted

Athena for the Parthenon, the god sat on a throne of gold, ebony, ivory, and precious stones, the base of which was carved with figures of Greek gods and mystical animals. The god's beard, hair, and robe were golden and his skin was made of ivory that had to be treated with oil kept in a special pool in the temple to prevent the humidity from cracking it. Zeus held a figure of Nike (Victory) in his right hand and an eagle-crowned scepter in the left. When the Christian emperor Theodosius I abolished the Olympic Games in 392 C.E., wealthy Greeks moved the statue to Constantinople, where a fire destroyed it in 462.

The *Temple of Artemis at Ephesus* was constructed on marshland in modern-day Turkey around 800 B.C.E. It had 127 Ionic-capitaled white marble columns extending to sixty feet in height. It was filled with bronze statues of the goddess sculpted by the finest artists of their day. One statue of a many-breasted Artemis survives to this day in the museum of Ephesus. Pilgrims from as far as Persia and India left offerings of gold and ivory statues and jewelry at the temple, which served as both a marketplace and a religious institution. The temple was destroyed by the invading Goths in 262 C.E.

The *Mausoleum at Halicarnassus* (353 C.E.) was a spectacular tomb in what is now southwest Turkey. The sarcophagus itself, built for the otherwise unremarkable King Mausollos, was of white alabaster decorated with gold. The edifice was topped by a pyramid, and contained many large statues of people, lions, horses, and other figures. It stood for sixteen centuries until an earthquake damaged it, and later the Knights of St. John of Malta used its marble blocks in other buildings nearby, where they can be seen today. Some of the sculptures also survive in the British Museum, but otherwise all that is left of Halicarnassus is the word we use today for an edifice housing the dead—mausoleum.

About 280 B.C.E. the *Colossus of Rhodes* was an enormous bronze statue of Helios, the Greek sun god, that stood guard over the harbor of the Mediterranean island of Rhodes. Completed in 282 B.C.E., an earthquake in 226 B.C.E. toppled it. It laid there broken for almost a thousand years until its disassembled remains were sold and transported to Syria on the backs of nine hundred camels.

Combining majesty with practicality, the Egyptians erected the *Lighthouse of Alexandria*, beginning in 290 B.C.E. This structure, the height of a modern forty-story building, was topped by a statue of the sea god Poseidon. Its light guided sailors into the harbor by means of a giant mirror that reflected sunlight during the day and fire at night. The reflection could be seen for thirty-five miles (100 km). It survived several earthquakes until one in 1323 crumbled it. In 1480 C.E. the Egyptian Mameloouk Sultan, Qaitbay, built a fort with the fallen stone and marble. Like other famous monuments, the lighthouse was depicted on Roman coins of the day. It was the last Ancient Wonder to disappear.

These ancient Pagan architectural and engineering models are equal in engineering ingenuity and aesthetic appeal to the Golden Gate Bridge, the Hoover Dam, the Sydney Opera House, and many other architectural wonders today.

See **Encyclopedia, Libraries, Olympic Games, Artemis, Nike, Hypatia, Hanging Gardens of Babylon.**

69

Smithcraft

The process of transforming stone and ore into metal and art is magical. Pagan gods preside over this magic and over the forge where this magic is performed. For example, Goibnu is the Irish god of smithcraft and Weyland ruled the smithcraft of the Norse. Tubal Cain was an ancient smith god who shaped metal at a forge near the Black Sea, while Greek smiths turn to Hephaestos and Romans to Vulcan, from whose name we get the word "volcano." Many Irish and other Western smiths call upon Bridget, goddess of inspiration and the forge, to guide their hands, especially when working with gold.

Prior to the advent of mining, late Neolithic people cold-shaped (not heated over a fire) nuggets of pure copper and gold found above ground. Since both copper and gold are relatively malleable metals, these nuggets were easily joined, shaped, and decorated. The earliest use of metal was probably for personal adornment, as a pendant found in a cave near Shanidar, Iraq, dating from 9500 B.C.E. and jewelry found at

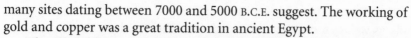

many sites dating between 7000 and 5000 B.C.E. suggest. The working of gold and copper was a great tradition in ancient Egypt.

The Chalcolithic, or copper and stone age, is the time when the technology of separating copper from ore was developed. Worked copper was easily portable and thus more utilitarian for commerce. For these reasons and for its qualities of being stronger than stone, all peoples exposed to copper readily accepted it as currency.

Metalworkers discovered that making alloys of copper and tin produced bronze, which was much harder and more durable than copper alone. The oldest hoard of copper and copper alloy artifacts, done by the lost-wax technique, was found in a cave on the shores of the Dead Sea and dated to 3600 B.C.E. Copper's quality of easily blending with other metals makes it the sacred metal of the love goddesses such as Greek Aphrodite, Roman Venus, Norse Freya, and African Yemaya.

Smithcraft is the working of metals. Blacksmiths work "black" metals such as iron, whereas whitesmiths work such "white" metals as silver, tin, and zinc. The development and application of knowledge and awareness of metals and their properties is more properly called metallurgy, which is concerned with the entire process from ore to finished product. The artisans who worked metals did so before there was a science of metallurgy.

Everywhere the smiths who worked the metal enjoyed high social standing. Ancient Scythian (present-day Ukraine) jewelers, for example, were renowned for their exquisite goldsmithing. In his workshop, called a smithy, the smith crafted furniture, weapons, and cooking utensils, as well as tools, gates, and sculpture. The smithy contained a forge, or hearth, for heating the metal until it was malleable, an anvil for shaping it, and a slack tub filled with water to cool and harden forged metal. His essential tools were tongs and hammer. Metal was shaped in other ways than by the force of the smith's hammer. Another method used to shape metal was pouring molten metal into hollow castings and piece molds. Lost-wax casting was done in the fourth millennium B.C.E. in Iraq. Sand casting was another method.

More recently, Etruscans, from the region of Italy now called Tuscany, left a twenty-five-hundred-year-old bronze tablet called Tabula Cortonensis. They created images of gold and bronze; vessels for holding water, wine, oil, or ashes have been found in Etruscan tombs.

Metalwork was not limited to Europe and the Near East, however. The Native Americans of the Upper Great Lakes region crafted copper tools 6,700 years ago. Inscriptions on metal objects matched motifs and designs on local rock art.

Our Pagan ancestors have left us a legacy of strength and beauty by learning how to work metal, as well as the deities who watch over those activities. They have also left many splendid works of metal such as armor, implements, and jewelry. From smiths to diamond cutters, all work with the blessings of the gods.

See **Coinage and Currency, Bridget.**

70

Spinning

The first concrete evidence that archaeologists Anne Stine Ingstad and Helge Ingstad found of a Viking presence in North America was a spindle whorl (a slender, rounded and tapered rod used in hand spinning). The Ingstads spent nearly a decade in the 1960s combing through what they thought might be the remnants of a Viking settlement at L'Anse aux Meadows on the coast of Newfoundland. It wasn't until they located the piece of the spinning wheel that they definitely knew they had found true traces of the Vinland settlement established by Leif Eriksson in about 998 C.E.

The spindle was more than just an artifact of a vanished civilization. Spindles—and spinning—have always loomed large in Pagan history and culture. A large number of goddesses from a variety of traditions are associated with spinning, and many Pagans consider spinning itself to be a magical act.

British-Celtic spinning goddess Habetrot is revered by folk who live along the English-Scottish border and in the Orkney Islands. Her spinning was believed to be so magical that anyone who wore clothing made from the fiber she spun would never get ill. In the Germanic tradition, Holda is the goddess who spins in a kingdom below the earth. Women who descended to Holda's world and worked diligently would return to the upperworld with their arms filled with gold.

Elsewhere, the Baltic sun goddess Saule spills out golden light as a gift to human beings when she spins her way across the sky every day. When the ancient Norse people looked up to the night sky, the line of stars that make up Orion's belt appeared to them as the goddess's spindle. That linear star spindle is associated with both Frigga and Freya. In ancient Egypt, the goddess Isis is credited with the invention of all domestic arts—including spinning—and giving them to humanity. Pallas Athena is the goddess in the Greek pantheon who brought the arts of weaving and spinning to the people. And the spinning wheel in the center of India's flag is a reference to that country's mother goddess who spun a web of cotton that stretched from one end of the country to the other.

Spinning, the art of gathering loose fibers together and twisting them into a thread or yarn, is probably most famously recalled in the story of Sleeping Beauty, as she pricked her finger and fell into a one-hundred-year sleep. Perhaps the most famous spinner is Rumpelstiltskin, who spun straw into gold for a queen and demanded her first-born son in return. The complication was that the queen could only keep her child if she managed to guess his name. Since this was a fairy tale in which everything comes right in the end, the queen guessed his name and triumphed.

In many folk tales throughout the world, only noble and industrious women can spin successfully. Sometimes there's even an element of self-sacrifice involved. In the famous story of the eleven wild swans, it is only through the willingness of their sister to perform the painful act of spinning stinging nettles into yarn and knitting that yarn into sweaters that the spell that has changed them into swans can be broken.

Spiders' magical ability to spin their webs are elements in many Pagan cosmologies. Arachne, for example, was a petulant Lydian princess transformed by Athena into a web-spinning spider. And Spiderwoman is the beloved North American spinning goddess belonging to the indigenous people of the American southwest.

See **The Fates, the Furies, and the Norns, The Wheel.**

71

Viking Long Ships

The famed "steeds of the sea" represent one of the greatest technological achievements of the Viking era. These sleek trim sturdy wooden longboats enabled Viking explorers and raiders to travel the known world, and far beyond. It is known that the ships reached across the Atlantic to northern Labrador, supposedly dubbed "Vinland," for the wild grapes that were found there. The Vikings were able to settle Iceland and Greenland, and while they continued trading with Europe or conquering it, they left a genetic mark as well: many of the redheads found in Ireland and the British Isles probably carry DNA from the Viking raiders and settlers. Likewise, the word "Russia" is believed to relate to the "rus" or red hair and beards of the Vikings who took the eastern route across the Baltic and down the rivers.

With regard to Russia, note that the Viking boats were light enough so that their raiders could push the boats across the land as they traversed a river system—to today's Black Sea. These shallow-draft ships could sail in relatively low water and could be drawn right up on the beach so warriors could jump out, raid, and quickly flee.

The ships are known today because of the Viking practice of ship burial in which eminent personages and their most significant possessions were placed in a ship and buried in a mound. Best known is the well-preserved Oseberg ship, which is the last resting place of Queen Asa, mother of King Halfdon the Black.

The Oseberg ship was found on a Norwegian farmer's land in 1908, and scholars date its construction to sometime around 800 C.E. The oak ship has the typical wooden keel that terminates in an elegant coiled-snake-curved prow at each end. The eighty-foot long ship has oar ports along its length and a wooden fish that supports the mast, which could be erected or laid flat even while the ship was at sea. Today the Oseberg ship is the centerpiece of Norway's Viking Ship Museum in an Oslo suburb.

Though the Oseberg ship has coiled snakes on its prows, many other Viking ships used intricately carved images of dragons or other fearsome beasts. So frightening was the approach of a dragon ship throughout Christian Europe, the phrase "from the wrath of the Norsemen, oh Lord protect us" was added to many liturgies in Christian churches.

The first documented Viking raid hit the Lindisfarne monastery on England's north coast in 794 C.E. Some Vikings were unabashed raiders, bringing sea chests filled with booty back to what are present-day Norway, Sweden, and Denmark; many others were peaceful traders and settlers looking for farmland.

Each Viking sailor kept his possessions in his own sea chest, which doubled as a rowing bench. And when they found favorable winds, they hoisted huge woolen sails woven by Viking women on upright looms. Like sailors from every other era, they left graffiti. Runic markings carved on a stone lion found in Venice and the balcony of the Hagia Sophia cathedral in Istanbul testify to the reach of the Viking ships.

72

The Wheel

The wheel is the central conceptual metaphor in many Pagan religions. Witches, ancient Pagans, NeoPagans, Heathens, and others celebrate Wheel of the Year—Spring, Summer, Autumn, and Winter—with rituals, gatherings, and festivities of all kinds at the solstices and equinoxes. Eastern peoples draw elaborate and intricate mandalas (circles representing the universe), many Native Americans create sacred circles marked by the four cardinal directions, and Europeans erect stone circles. Lady Luck spins the Wheel of Fortune.

Contemporary Witches honor the Wheel of Life, which begins with birth and continues through initiation, consummation, and repose, and ends with death. Initiation can be a young woman's first blood, a male's formal or informal initiation into manhood, or it can be a spiritual initiation into a religious group or a formal spiritual path shared with others (the Jewish bar mitzvah serves both purposes). Consummation can be marriage or the first experience of sexual intercourse. Repose is something women find after years spent giving birth to and rearing children—no longer of reproductive age, but not yet ready to leave this world of the living. For men and women alike, repose may be when they have attained career goals and can relax and enjoy them. The wheel has no ending and no beginning; the religious significance of the Wheel of Life is its endlessness: from death comes birth again.

There would be no civilization as we know it without the wheel. No spinning of thread or grinding of corn or shaping of pots, no carts or trains or spaceships. The earliest evidence of wheels is an ancient drawing found in a cave in the present Czech Republic dating from ten thousand years ago; it shows the stick figure of a man apparently rolling a round object and knocking over two other stick people. Archaeologist Dmitri Szawjk interprets this, and other drawings of wheels and people found in the same cave, as saying something like, "Wheel good. Have wheel;t.;t.;t.;tdefeat others." Another drawing shows a person with two horns on his head standing near a wheel with his arms up in an attitude of rejoicing. A third shows two dancing men with erect penises holding their hands up toward a wheel. This could be the sun, and might be related to the Norse sun wheel that's such an important symbol for Heathens of yore and those of today.

Although the drawings in the Czech cave are about two thousand years older, the peoples of ancient Mesopotamia are usually credited with inventing the first wheel. Estimates date its invention range from 5500 to 3000 B.C.E., with most guesses around 4000. The oldest artifacts in the Middle East show wheels dating from 3000 B.C.E., although the wheel could have been in use earlier. The oldest surviving goblets also date from the same time. Perhaps this signifies that wheels were used for pottery making before they were used for transportation. The wheel was invented independently in China around 2800 B.C.E. Wheel-like worked stones have been found in Incan and other western hemisphere cultures from about 1500 B.C.E. The Sumerians built two-wheeled chariots around 3500 B.C.E. They already had domesticated horses and oxen. By hitching horses to chariots, they were able to travel greater distances faster and more easily. Then by adding two more wheels to make carts and wagons, they unburdened the shoulders of the common man from carrying supplies and equipment.

The wheel's invention not only revolutionized transportation and pottery manufacture, but also improved other arts and technologies such as spinning. Spinners adapted the wheel for spinning fibers into yarn, and ancient hydraulic engineers used wheels to create the pulleys that lifted the buckets to water the fabled Hanging Gardens of Babylon over three thousand years ago.

The cranking of a wheel causes the hurdy-gurdy to sing; the spinning of prayer wheels carries our prayers to the gods; the casting of a sacred circle creates a macrocosmic world. Every circle dance is a magical act imitating the great wheel of life, the round of the seasons, the spinning of Earth. And that, dear reader, is Pagan.

See **Pottery, Spinning, Hanging Gardens of Babylon.**

73

The Witches' Voice

Pagans have had a prominent and highly visible presence on the World Wide Web since its inception. In fact, many Pagans earn their living working in the computer industry, where they design programs, spin websites, compose music, broadcast news and opinions, and perform all functions associated with electronic communication.

Witches, Druids, recons (reconstructed traditions such as Celtic Recon, Hellenic Recon, etc.), and other Pagan practitioners are well represented on several general religious sites as well as in local, regional, and international interfaith communities. Two important general religious sites are www.tolerance.org, a Web project of the Southern Poverty Law Center, and www.religioustolerance.org, sponsored by the Ontario Consultants on Religious Tolerance. Beliefnet (www.beliefnet.com) publishes current writings by people of all faith traditions, but specifically engages several Pagan authors to write columns.

Thousands, possibly millions, of Pagans regularly participate in online discussions via listservs; create and maintain personal and organizational websites; network with each other and with people of other religions; do research; and even perform ritual (cyberritual) and spellwork (cybermagic) online.

But most important to Pagans is a website begun in 1996 by two Massachusetts Witches, Wren Walker and Fritz Jung. Their mission was "to promote tolerance" and to rectify "many of the misconceptions related to the modern Witch/Wiccan/Pagan movement." Shortly after mounting their first three pages on the Internet for Laurie Cabot's Witches League for Public Awareness (WLPA), the couple moved to Florida, obtained the domain name Witchvox, and launched The Witches' Voice (TWV or Witchvox, www.witchvox.com). Witchvox has grown beyond anybody's expectations since its debut on February 2, 1997 (a sabbat called, variously, Imbolg, Candlemas, or Brigit), "with fifty-six pages and some new technology for the links and contacts section." During all this time they have provided a free, neutral, and inclusive forum for Pagans, Heathens, Witches, and Wiccans.

The owners, Fritz and Wren, do not accept any advertising, although TWV is incorporated as a religious institution and carries a 501(c)(3) that allows tax-deductible donations to help cover hosting expenses, software, and so forth. A small crew of volunteers helps with the site work.

One of TWV's most important services is The Wren's Nest, which posts news of interest to Pagans and Witches from sources worldwide. The Wren's Nest currently contains nine thousand news clips that help keep activists, history buffs, and amateur archaeologists informed. In

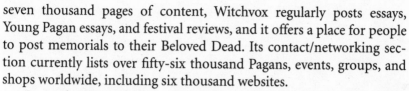

seven thousand pages of content, Witchvox regularly posts essays, Young Pagan essays, and festival reviews, and it offers a place for people to post memorials to their Beloved Dead. Its contact/networking section currently lists over fifty-six thousand Pagans, events, groups, and shops worldwide, including six thousand websites.

In a phenomenal feat of devotion, Witchvox's fans garnered a Webby Award (the Internet equivalent of an Oscar) in the Spirituality category for their beloved site in July 2003 by going online and doing a write-in vote, thus tallying for Witchvox more votes than Beliefnet, The Vatican's, or Grace Cathedral's websites.

Since its founding in 1997, The Witches' Voice has grown to become the most popular Pagan site on the World Wide Web. It broke 100 million actual pages viewed/requested from seekers from all over the world (nearly 370 million "hits") by Yule (December) 2003.

V

MYTHOLOGICAL PERSONAGES

As we've seen throughout this book, mythology and folklore offer us our major resources for Pagan thought, belief, and practices. We in the contemporary Western world are familiar with the myths and tales of these gods and mortals, particularly those from the Greco-Roman world. We speak of "Herculean tasks," "the hounds of Hekate," and the pipes of Pan. Aphrodite and Mercury, Bacchus with his grapes, and shy, slim Diana of the beasts—these personages, and many more, play a large role in our everyday lives and understandings. They form the basis of much of our common culture; they influence us more than we realize. Many of us even name our children for these divine entities. How many Dianas do you know?

74

Aphrodite

Aphrodite is one of the most popular and best-loved goddesses of all times and all places, for she is the goddess of love. Aphrodite Nymphia reigns in the bridal chamber; Aphrodite Melainis means black or sex after dark; and Aphrodite Praxis, meaning sexual action, is the name of an ivory image of her in her temple at Athens. She is called Aphrodite Morpho, "of shapely form" and she is also the Postponer of Old Age. The playwright Euripides said, "Do you not see how mighty is the goddess Aphrodite? She sows and gives that love from which all we upon this earth are born."

There are three different stories about Aphrodite's birth. The Greek poet Homer, among others, believed she was the daughter of Zeus and a woman named Dione, although which of more than one Dione is unclear. In another story, a large egg fell into the Euphrates River, a fish rolled it to the bank, and doves sat on it until it hatched Aphrodite. Interestingly, white doves, such as those used to decorate wedding cakes, are her sacred birds. The most famous story of the birth of Aphrodite, however, says that when the Titan Cronos ("Time") cut off the genitals of his father Uranus ("Sky") with an adamantine sickle and threw them into the sea, the beautiful Aphrodite sprang from the foam. This account, told by the Greek poet Hesiod circa 700 B.C.E., makes Aphrodite the oldest of the Olympians.

The best-known illustration of this divine genesis is a painting done in 1485 C.E. by a Florentine Renaissance painter Sandro Botticelli called "The Birth of Venus" (Venus is Aphrodite's Roman name). It shows a delicate woman emerging from the sea on a cockle shell being wafted ashore by wind gods amidst a shower of roses. This representation of foam-born Aphrodite is jestingly called "Venus on the half shell," and reproductions of it in both two- and three-dimensional media can be found on many NeoPagan altars. More than thirteen hundred years earlier in 130–120 B.C.E. Rome, an anonymous sculptor carved the goddess' image in marble. This statue, now in the Musée de Louvre in Paris, is known as "Venus de Milo."

Aphrodite was married to Hephaestus, the lame god of smiths, but it was to the war god Ares that she gave her heart. Although Aphrodite had none by her husband Hephaestus, she had several children. By Ares she bore three: Deimos, Phobus ("Fear and Panic"), and Harmonia. With divine Dionysus of the vine she is said to have given birth to Priapus, known primarily for his enormous penis. Aphrodite's union with Hermes, the messenger, traveler, and thief, produced Hermaphroditus, born male but later changed to half male, half female. Among her mortal lovers was Anchises, with whom Aphrodite had Aeneas, hero of Troy and of Virgil's epic *Aeneid*. There are also tales of Aphrodite's love affairs with Adonis, Eros, and others.

However, the most famous story of Aphrodite, sung of by Homer in the *Iliad*, concerns the part she played in the Judgment of Paris and the ensuing ten-year war between the Greeks (Acheans) and Troy.

Like Inanna and Ishtar in Mesopotamia and Syrian Astarte, Aphrodite is the morning and the evening star, which is the planet Venus. Perhaps this is because early morning and evening are popular hours for lovemaking. Her sacred colors are red and pink; love tokens such as Valentine cards are made in red and pink, with lace trimming like the foam from which Aphrodite first emerged from the sea. Roses, Aphrodite's sacred flowers, are traditionally given as a token of love, and along with her white doves they also adorn wedding cakes. Pearls from the sea are her sacred jewels, and they, too, decorate wedding cakes and are traditionally worn by brides or sewn onto bridal gowns. Friday (Vendredi, or Venus' day, in French) is her sacred day. Her sacred metal is copper, that metal which most readily forms alloys with other metals just as Venus becomes one with her lovers. The most efficacious love spells are those initiated on Friday, and copper pennies, pearls, rose petals and rose oil, red or pink candles, and red cloth are nearly always used in such magic.

Today, Venus is still sung about in popular music. Madison Avenue uses the goddess to sell women's razors of the same name. Despite this ignominy, however, mighty Aphrodite is loved and worshipped by contemporary Pagans just as she was in her earliest cults in Assyria, Cyprus, Palestine, and other countries in the Mediterranean basin.

See **The *Iliad*.**

75

Artemis

The Artemis of the Greek Olympians walks with many women today. Although her worship isn't limited to females, it is to women that Artemis speaks most ardently. She is known for keeping men away, for those who would remain maidens. A story is told of Artemis and Callisto, the maid who had sworn to remain a virgin, which suggests that Artemis's love of women had a romantic and sexual dimension. However, when Zeus, in one of his frequent randy moods, assumes the shape of Artemis, he is able to seduce and impregnate Callisto. When Artemis sees Callisto's swelling belly, she knows Callisto has broken her pledge. Callisto says it's the goddess's fault. This angers Artemis and she changes Callisto into a bear.

The Greek lexicon-encylopedia *Suidas* tells of a cult in Athens where, in celebration of a festival for Artemis, young girls between the ages of five and ten years played the bear (Arktos) in her honor. These saffron-robed virgins were called *arctoi*. The practice comes from a time when young girls tamed a wild she-bear and played with it. And the temple of the goddess Artemis Proseoia at Euboia, Greece, surrounded by trees and enclosed by upright slabs of pure white marble, has the strange quality of giving off the color and odor of saffron when rubbed with the hand.

At Arkadia, the goddess, whose symbol is the New Moon (the slender maiden moon), is worshipped as Artemis Hymnia (of hymns). Only virginal priestesses could serve her there but in later years post-menopausal priestesses presided. Suidas tells us that "virgins about to have sex dedicated their virginal lingerie to Artemis," more evidence of Artemis's connection with young women. The proper crown of flowers for Artemisian rites was one made of blossoms from a virgin meadow, one far away from people, and the customary time to honor her is during her sacred month of May.

One of her names is Artemis Hêmerasia, meaning "she who soothes." Besides favoring young girls, Artemis assists women in childbirth and heals and protects babies and young children. Women in labor call to Artemis Ilythia (Eileithyia) for release as in the Orphic Hymn to Prothyraia:

"O venerable Goddess, hear my prayer, for labour pains are thy peculiar care ... With births you sympathise, though pleased to see the numerous offspring of fertility. When racked with labour pangs, and sore distressed the sex invoke thee, as the soul's sure rest; for thou Eileithyia alone canst give relief to pain, which art attempts to ease, but tries in vain. Artemis Eileithyia, venerable power, who bringest relief in labour's dreadful hour; hear, Prothyraia and make the infant race thy constant care."

A statue of Artemis stands guardian of the sanctuary of Asklepios at Sykyon, and a sanctuary of the physician Asklepios at Messene contains statues of the Muses, Artemis's brother Apollo, and Artemis Phosphoros ("Bringer of Light"), as further evidence of her strong connection with healing and health. As protectress, Artemis is watcher over streets and harbors. As they have for thousands of years, women today call upon the strength and protection of Artemis when walking the streets at night.

Born on the island of Delos just before her twin brother Apollo, Artemis is mistress of the whole of wild nature. She is called Lady of the Beasts and Queen of Animals. Frequently, she is portrayed in a hunting posture: hurling a javelin (Artemis Aitolia), carrying torches, or shooting one of her golden arrows that can bring disease and death if the goddess is angered. This slender, swift-footed maiden goddess, with her quiver on her shoulder and bow in hand, roams the wilds with her hunting dogs. Hunters seek the blessings of Artemis Agrotera (the huntress). As goddess of the wilds, she is associated with certain trees—laurel, cedar, walnut—and animals—deer, wolves, goats. Artemisia, her sacred herb, brings dreams and visions.

Artemis's temples, sacred groves, and white (for its purity) marble statues were spread in cities and in the remotest places all around Greece, and beyond—at Corinth, Megaris, Sparta, Arkadia, Lydia, Phrygia, Ephesos, Thessaly, and as far as Italia, as well as the islands of Delos, Crete, and Rhodes. These are also the cities where her cults were recognized. Statues of Artemis also stood in and around the Gymnasia at Elis where the Olympic Games were held. The best-known statue of Artemis (Diana), called "Diana of Versailles," belongs to the collection of the Louvre in Paris. This is a Roman marble adaptation of a fourth-century B.C.E. Greek cult statue by Leokhares that shows her wearing a light tunic, with hair bound, and stepping forward on her left foot, while her right hand reaches over her shoulder to her quiver and her left rests upon the head of a deer. There is a replica of this statue in Sutro Park in San Francisco, where modern Pagans assemble for ritual. This Diana—for here she is called by her Roman name—is frequently anointed and adorned with fresh flower offerings, evidence of her worship today. The best way to honor Artemis is to care for the natural world. Clean up pollution, protect wildlife, donate time and money to ecological concerns. But don't just do it from your safe cities: actually get out into the wild, and experience the natural world.

After running with animals all day, the goddess likes to return to Apollo's house at Delphi, where, as Artemis Hêgemonê (leader), she leads the dance of the Muses and the Charites (Charities).

See **The Muses, Asclepius.**

76

Bridget

To the Celts the goddess Bridget is three sisters and she is one. Goddess of the forge and smithcraft, of poetry, and of healing. Her name has many variations: Brigit, Brighid, Bride or Bridey, Brigandu, Brigantia, among others. As *Brei-Sauggead* ("fiery arrow"), she is described as having flame red hair rising from her head. As *Brighid bhoidheach* ("Bride the beautiful"), she inspires the poet. Her healing waters rise from sacred springs throughout Ireland; the sick go to the springs to pray and leave offerings and seek cures for illness and injury. Her worship goes back before memory.

Bridey can whistle up the wind on a still day. She taught humans how to keep bees and to brew mead from their honey. She brought the art of keening for the dead.

At her ancient shrine at Kildare in Ireland, nineteen women tended the sacred flame of Bridget. The church ordered her flame extinguished about four hundred years ago, claiming it was a Pagan practice, and the nuns dispersed. Then in the late twentieth century one of the sisters in the order received a message from Bridget that it was time to return to Kildare and relight the flame. This was accomplished in 1993. Since then, as of old, each woman keeps the flame for a day for one of the nineteen days and on the twentieth, the goddess herself tends it.

We celebrate her holy day on February 2, called Bridget, Imbolc ("the lambing season" or "in the belly") or Candlemas, when the light is returning and Earth is warming. White flowers spring up in Bridget's footsteps. We gather rushes and weave Bridget's crosses to hang over our doorways to remind us of her blessings of the coming year. Bridget is the season to review our past, to emerge from the indoors and the darkness, and step again out into the world of lightness. It is the time to pledge ourselves to new projects or new ways of being, to rededicate ourselves to Bridey. We relight our candles from her flame. We dress a straw Bridey (like a bride) dolly in white lace and flowers and follow her in a spiral dance of renewal. Also each year in the first week of February pilgrims of all religions come to Kildare for her festival.

Bridget has traveled throughout the world, and today her worship even extends into cyberspace, where exists an online sister- and brotherhood called Ord Brighideach. Worshippers of the goddess take twenty-four-hour shifts of keeping her flame. Flamekeepers are grouped into cells named for trees, comprising three hundred flamekeepers in twelve countries.

Bridey's brightness warms the hearts of all.

See **Brewing, Corn Dollies.**

77

Demeter & Persephone/Kore

One of the most beautiful and enduring stories in the Western world is about a mother's love for her daughter. It speaks powerfully to the deepest part of self—of the cycles of life, of changes and transformations, of darkness and light. Demeter, "barley mother," goddess of health, birth, and marriage, loses her daughter, Persephone, sometimes called Kore (maiden) when the latter is frolicking in the meadow with her girlfriends, picking crocuses and lilies. When Kore strays out of sight, Hades, stern god of the Underworld, abducts the maid and takes her away in his chariot. The only witnesses to the kidnap are Helios, the sun, who sees everything, and Hekate, who seldom stayed around Olympus with the other gods, preferring instead to wander.

When Demeter discovers her daughter missing, she roams Earth calling in vain for Persephone. For nine days and nights Demeter wanders. She won't eat, she won't sleep, she won't bathe. On the tenth day Hekate tells Demeter she'd heard the abduction and Helios tells her where it happened, but that Zeus had told Hades to take the girl.

So Demeter refuses the company of the gods and instead goes about with the people of the towns and fields. There are many stories of Demeter's experiences during this time. Disguised as an old woman, she walks to Eleusis and offers herself for domestic work. When eventual circumstances cause her to reveal herself to mortals, she straightens her spine, the lines fade from her face, and gray disappears from her hair.

Meanwhile, Persephone eats seven seeds of the pomegranate, which means she has tasted the secrets of the Underworld and cannot leave. Demeter still grieves the loss of her precious daughter. She causes the plows to break, destroys the cattle, makes barren the fields, and blights the seed. She brings famine to all of Earth.

The gods hold a council to figure out what to do. Zeus sends Hermes to Hades to fetch Persephone back to her mother. But because Persephone has eaten of the pomegranate, she is bound to Hades. Either the planet Earth and everyone on it dies because of Demeter's grief, or the gods have to come up with some other solution. Zeus works out a deal among the gods, Demeter and Hades, that Persephone will spend part of each year in the Underworld and part on Earth with her mother. When Persephone is upon Earth, Demeter, in her joy, causes the grain to grow and ripen, the flowers to bloom, the sweet fruits to drop. And when Persephone returns to the dark realm she rules, the growing things wither and die. Our experience of the seasons of the year reflect Demeter's alternating grief and joy.

Demeter continues to reveal herself to mortals, usually near her cult center at Eleusis. Eleusis, near Athens, is the site where pilgrims gathered each year to be initiated into Demeter's mysteries. For instance, there is a story of a traveler on a bus to Eleusis just after World War II. An old woman gets on the bus. She hasn't the fare. The traveler pays the fare. She disappears and the traveler soon comes into wealth, a gift from the grateful Demeter.

Re-creations of the Eleusinian Mysteries take place annually in many places far from Greece, as Witches, Hellenic reconstructionists, and other NeoPagans partake in the ancient mysteries of death and rebirth.

See **Hekate, the Goddess of the Witches, Mercury/Hermes.**

78

Dionysus

The Greek Dionysus, called Bacchus or Liber ("the free one") by the Romans, is the god of wine. For the wandering hero Odysseus the god was "the best source of life for mortals." Considered an exceptionally attractive young man, Dionysus gives pleasure to humankind. He appears wearing fox or deerskin, and in war, panther skins.

Most of what we know about him comes from Greek and Roman sources, which link him with the gods of Olympus. Other appellations attached to Dionysus are Bromios, meaning "thunderer" or "he of the loud shout"; Dendrites, "he of the trees"; Eleutherios, "the liberator"; Lenaeus of the wine press; Liknites "he of the winnowing fan" associated with fertility; and Lyaeus, "he who releases," who gives relaxation and freedom from worry. These are all qualities of his sacred wine. Another name is Dithyrambos, "he of the double door," which refers both to songs sung to him during his festival and to the strange circumstances of his double birth.

One version of Dionysus's birth says that he is the son of the mortal Semele and the god Zeus. There are two explanations for why Dionysus is called twice born. One story concerns the jealousy of Zeus's wife, Hera, and her plot to eliminate her rival for his affections. Hera urges Semele to get Zeus to reveal himself to her in all his divinity. Mortals cannot look upon a god without dying, so when Zeus complies, Semele is struck by a thunderbolt, at which point she gives birth to Dionysus prematurely and then dies. Zeus sews the fetus up in his thigh and gives birth to him when gestation is complete.

In an alternate story, Dionysus is the child of two divinities, Zeus and Persephone. A jealous Hera convinces the elder gods, the Titans, to dismember Dionysus, but Zeus fights them off using thunderbolts. Unfortunately, by the time Zeus succeeds, the heart of Dionysus is the only part of him left. According to different versions Zeus either implants the heart in the womb of Semele or he gives it to her to eat. In either case, Semele gives Dionysus a "second birth."

It is also said that Hera struck Dionysus with madness and set him to wander the countryside. He wound up in Phrygia, where the goddess Rhea healed him and taught him secret rites. Either Rhea taught him, or Dionysus discovered on his own the culture of the vine and the mode of extracting its precious juice. Rhea is also said to have sent him off to teach viticulture (the cultivation of grapevines) as far afield as India.

There came to be mystery cults dedicated to Dionysus. In Thrace his communicants were called Bassarids, referring to the fox skin Dionysus often wore, symbolizing new life. His worship took place in secret groves and wild places, with celebrants drinking to excess, eating raw meat, and dancing in ecstasy (from the Greek word *ekstasis*, meaning "to drive out" of the stasis, out of ordinary consciousness). Worshippers were women only, called Maenads, meaning "raving ones." They dressed in fawn skin, with the sacred ivy and vines of Dionysus in their disheveled hair, and carried the thyrsus (a staff covered in pine cones, vines, and ivy leaves). Among his nonhuman followers were satyrs, half-man half-goat nature spirits that haunted the woods and mountains, always with erect phalli; centaurs, creatures with human heads and torsos, and the body of a horse; and sileni, also half-man and half-horse, but bald and fat with thick lips, squat noses, and the ears of a horse.

The first theatrical performances in ancient Greece were revelries in honor of Dionysus, and included the singing of Dithyrambos (odes and hymns to the god). His cult was introduced to Rome around 200 B.C.E., where it was called the Bacchanalia and the worshippers called Bacchantes, for his Roman name of Bacchus. The rites lasted for three days and nights in mid-March.

Another story tells of Dionysus either hiring a pirate ship to take him to the Greek island of Naxos or being kidnapped by sailors for their sexual pleasures. The sailors try to take him to Asia to sell him as a slave, but the god turns the mast and oars into snakes and fills the ship with ivy and the sound of flutes. This drives sailors mad, so they leap into the sea, where Dionysus turns them into dolphins.

In another myth, Dionysus is the god who grants King Midas the gift of the golden touch, by which everything the king touches, including his beloved daughter and the food he attempts to eat, turns to gold. Midas, recognizing his mistake, begs Dionysus to take back the gift and deliver him from starvation. Dionysus then tells Midas to wash in the river Pactolus. When Midas touches the waters, power passes into them, and that's why the sands of Pactolus are full of gold.

Dionysus coupled with many females and fathered many children. Three of his sons by Ariadne were among the Argonauts who sailed with Jason in his quest for the Golden Fleece. By the goddess Aphrodite, he sired the Charites: Aglaea, Euphrosyne, and Thalia. Dionysus and Ariadne also produced Hymenaios, god of weddings, from whose name we take our word hymen, and Priapus, the protector of livestock, fruit plants, gardens, and male genitalia, always shown with large, ithyphallic genitalia.

There is evidence that the god known to the Greeks and Romans had a widespread cult following before the Olympic gods existed. Dionysus is the original *khristos*, the god who transforms those worshippers who imbibe him, the god you experience by eating him. The Christian sacrament of eating the symbolic blood and body of their god is an example of khristos. In this sense, the wine of the divine Dionysus is an entheogen, or a substance that gives presence of the god, or god intoxication. The use of entheogens, wine among them, is an important part of the religious rites of many contemporary Pagans.

See **Aphrodite, Theater, The *Odyssey*.**

79

The Fates, the Furies, and the Norns

Our Pagan ancestors believed their lives were fated. The Greek and the Norse peoples both had goddesses or female spirits who spun our fate. We are probably most familiar with the Greek goddesses, three sisters called the Fates. Their names are Clotho (or Clothos), who sings of the things that are; Atropus (Atropos), who sings of things that will be; and their sister Lachesis, as the apportioner of lots, who sings of things that were. All are seemingly connected with the textile arts, for one is a spinner, another a weaver, and the third cuts the thread of life. The Greeks called them the *Moerae*. Their mother is *Ananke*, "Necessity," the goddess of bonds, who rules compulsion, restraint, or coercion; she presides over all the ties of life, be they bonds of kinship, friendship, love, or master and slave. The Fates sing in unison with the music of the Sirens, part bird, part woman sea nymphs who lure unwary sailors to their island home with their song.

For the Greeks, Fate is ultimately death, for no one can escape it. But the interlaced designs of the sisters' fabric are not easy for mortals to understand. For this reason, many people consult oracles. And although the gods may interfere with the lives of humans, they cannot change the decisions of the Moerae as to the limit of a mortal's life span. For this reason the sisters have been called mighty, compelling, and overwhelming.

Three Greek nature spirits called the *Erinyes*, or Furies, seem to work in concert with the Moerae. Detecting and avenging crime and wickedness, the Erinyes assist the Moerae in steering the Ananke ("Necessity"—compulsion, restraint, or coercion and the bonds of life).

Born of Gaia (Earth) from the bloody drops of the Titan Uranus's severed genitals, the Erinyes, like the Moerae, are sisters. Alecto, the "unceasing one," is a spirit who revels in war and quarrels and is a maker of grief. Her sister Megaera is "She Who Holds a Grudge." The third, Tisiphone, is the avenger of murder who sits wrapped in a bloodstained robe guarding the entrance of Tartarus (the Underworld place of punishment). They are depicted with wings and sometimes with snakes in their hair, like the Gorgons.

Far from the eastern Mediterranean, in the north countries of Scandinavia, three other female figures determine the lives of mortals. Like their Greek cousins, they are sisters: Urd, "fate"; Verdandi, "necessity"; and Skuld, "being." The Norns are seen as crones who weave their tapestry at the base of the world tree Yggdrasil, controlling the destinies of men, gods, and the unchanging laws of the cosmos. They are the *disir* (female protective spirits) who assist women in labor and delivery; they also measure each life and allot its path from the moment of birth. To this day, Norwegians have a custom of making *nornegrauten* (literally "porridge of the Norns") upon the birth of a child.

Many NeoPagans respect and honor these ancestral goddesses, intent on living a life true to that decreed by the Fates.

See **Spinning, Yggdrasil, Oracles and Seers.**

80

Hekate, the Goddess of the Witches

Hekate is one of the oldest goddesses known by name. There are many different legends, going back to at least 700 B.C.E., of her parentage; it seems likely that as different people adopted her worship, the circumstances of her birth changed. She most likely originated in southwest Asia Minor, and only later, in the sixth century B.C.E., was she integrated into Greek religion. Although her worship preceded the arrival of the gods of Olympus, and she is sometimes considered to have been one of the earlier Titans, the Olympians accepted Hekate. She was not of their kind and never lived among them on Mount Olympus, for she was a goddess of Earth rather than the rarified heights.

The goddess' title of Hekate Chthonia comes from the Greek word *khthonios*, meaning "under the earth." Unlike the Olympians found in the upper regions, chthonic deities are concerned with basic living matters such as fertility, childbirth, fate, and death. Their altars are generally placed low to the ground, where offerings are poured into the ground. Creatures of darkness and Earth, those connected with chthonic powers—

ravens, owls, crows, snakes—are especially sacred to Hekate. She can take the form of a three-headed dog, horse, bear, or lion and is especially associated with black dogs called "the hounds of Hekate." The Roman poet Ovid says that she can be conjured from the darkness "with long howls." Virgil, in the *Aeneid*, describes the circumstances of her arrival:

> *The Earth began to bellow, trees to dance*
> *And howling dogs in glimmering light advance*
> *Ere Hekate came.*

Hekate presides over liminal realms. She is a goddess of both childbirth and death, both being transitions from and to another world. The amphibious frog, able to live on water and land, is another creature sacred to Hekate, probably in connection with her ruling over childbirth.

Legend has it that Hekate granted the Cumaen Sybil the power to control and tend the Avernus Wood, which hides a passageway into the Underworld. It is there that the Trojan hero Aeneas, with Sybil's help, was able to travel to the Underworld to commune with his dead father as well as his dead lover, Dido.

As Hekate Trivia ("three ways," from which we get the word "trivia"), she presides at the place where three roads meet. Ancient Greeks erected statues called *hecataea* at such crossroads, to honor her and to ensure her protection. This is the place where Witches meet to learn her mysteries. As guardian she is called Hekate Propylaia (root of our word "prophylactic"), and her statues guarded gateways, the entrances to the Acropolis in Athens, and the homes of the common people.

At Hekate's Suppers and at liminal realms such as trivia and sacred groves, it is appropriate for petitioners to leave offerings. She likes red mullet (fish that was forbidden in other cults), sprat, breadstuffs, raw eggs, cheese, garlic, cake, and honey. From my own experience, I know that sardines and wine please her. She especially likes the little round cakes decorated with miniature torches called *amphiphôn*. When you leave these offerings at the crossroads, don't look back.

She may appear as maiden or crone, and, as triple goddess, Hekate is often associated with Demeter and Persephone. Together, the three goddesses are seen as the three phases of the moon: Persephone the maiden is the New Moon; Demeter the mother, Full Moon; and Hekate, the Dark or waning Moon. She is often portrayed as having three faces facing in three directions, and three is her sacred number. She may carry a torch, with which she lights the way into the unknown darkness, or a knife to cut the cord of birth and death. This may be the origin of the Witch's sacred two-sided athame, since Hekate has always been called the Goddess of the Witches. She also may be shown carrying a rope or scourge, a key, a phial, flowers, or a pomegranate.

Trees sacred to Hekate are the yew, cypress, hazel, and willow. Willow contains the same fever reducer, salicylic acid, used in aspirin today. Hekate's sacred groves were of yew, a tree associated with the Under- world, death, and rebirth, because it resurrects itself by growing new trees from the rotting core of a dead trunk. Yew wood was commonly used to make dagger hilts and bows, a poison prepared from the seeds of the yew was used to make deadly arrow tips. The goddess's power is in the yew berry, a poison that can bring death or wisdom, depending on its careful preparation.

Among the herbs associated with Hekate, and used in her magical potions, are mugwort, cardamom, myrrh, lavender, almonds, garlic, hellebore, and mint. Tea made of dandelion, also sacred to Hekate, enhances psychic ability and helps people to contact the spirit world. Poisons and hallucinogens such as magic mushroom, opium poppy, hemlock, belladonna, mandrake, aconite (also known as hecateis, monkshood, or wolfsbane) are sacred to Hekate as well. Belladonna, mandrake, and aconite are ingredients in Witches' flying ointment. These ingredients must be prepared and blended very carefully in order to ensure their efficacy and to avoid poisoning.

In her spell-making roles, Hekate is called a sorceress, or maker of spells. The Greek word for sorceress is *Pharmakis*. Modern pharmacists who blend ingredients into medications are practicing alchemical transformation and making healing spells in the spirit of Hekate. If you only honor Hekate once a year, let that night be on November 16, Hekate Night. She is also traditionally worshipped on the eve of a new moon or the thirtieth of the month at Hekate's Suppers. These suppers may be held in her temples or in sacred groves dedicated to her. In ancient times such groves and temples were maintained by ritually castrated and transgendered priests of Hekate, called *Semnotatoi*. Priests and priestesses of Hekate cast horoscopes and created spells. Because she sometimes is called the "maid of the ruddy feet," many of her worshippers colored their hands and feet with henna. Athenian worshippers invoked her at midnight rituals, and midnight is still known as "the Witching hour," Hekate's hour.

See **Cumaean Sybil, Demeter and Persephone/Kore, The *Aeneid*, Oracles and Seers.**

81

Isis and Osiris

The legend of the goddess Isis and her consort Osiris is one of the most powerful tales from Egyptian mythology. Echoes of their tale are heard in Sumerian, Hindu, and Christian lore as well. Osiris teaches the arts of wine making and agriculture to the inhabitants of the Nile Valley, where he is much loved. His envious brother Set, god of strength, war, storms, foreign lands, and deserts, conspires to kill Osiris. Set first attempts to kill his brother by constructing a coffin exactly the right size for Osiris to fit in, then inviting the person it fit to claim it. As soon as Osiris lies in the coffin, Set slams it shut and throws it into the Nile River. The drowning of Osiris symbolizes the annual flooding of the river.

His lover, the goddess Isis and her sister Nephthys, goddess of the Underworld and childbirth, revive Osiris with their magic spells. But Set attacks Osiris again, and cuts him into thirteen pieces that he hides throughout the land. The grieving Isis seeks high and low for many years to find the parts. Finally, she finds all but one piece, so she puts Osiris's parts back together without it. Even without this part, she is able to bring him back to life temporarily and to become pregnant by him. Eventually Osiris dies again and descends to rule the Underworld.

The hawk-headed Horus, son of their divine union, who is secretly reared in the marshes, seeks vengeance for his uncle's fratricide. In the violent battle between nephew and uncle that ensues, Horus loses an eye and Set a testicle. For his crimes, the other gods exile Set to the hinterlands.

The legends of Isis and Osiris resemble the legends of the Sumerian goddess Inanna and her lover Dumuzi. As the drowning of Osiris causes the Nile's annual flooding, similarly the copulation of the Mesopotamian lovers brings the annual flooding of the Tigris and Euphrates Rivers, making the valleys fertile for the coming year's crops. In both cases, the lives of the gods affect the well-being and prosperity of the land and its people. And just as Isis revives the dead Osiris and becomes impregnated by him, so too the Hindu goddess Kali dances over the corpse of Shiva, arousing him to intercourse. Yet another primal human theme threads through these stories: ancient statues of Isis show her nursing her son Horus, like depictions of the Christian Mary, "Mother of God," holding her son/Sun, Jesus. Every goddess worshipper and Witch, not to mention every mother, appreciates, and even adores, this divine mother/son dyad.

See **The Descent of Inanna.**

82

Mercury/Hermes

Mercury is not a god who's been lost to the past. Indeed, today we see him everywhere. As god of communication and speech, he has lent his name and qualities to newspapers (the *San Jose Mercury News*), record labels (Mercury Records), broadcast and theater companies (Orson Welles's Mercury Theatre of the Air). Mercury, who was known as Hermes to the Greeks, is the archetypal magician. For example, Hermes gave wandering Odysseus a magic potion to make him immune to Circe's spells of seduction; and he taught Pandora the art of persuasion.

We recognize Mercury in his broad-brimmed winged cap called *petasos* and his winged sandals (*talaria*), indicative of his keenness of wit and swiftness of foot, even though he wears the humble clothing of a worker, traveler, or shepherd. His magical helmet has the power of rendering him invisible, signifying hidden thoughts and secrets. He carries the caduceus, the staff of herald and messenger of the gods, and a purse, showing him to be patron of merchants and traders, for from his name we get the words merchant and mercantile.

Around 495 B.C.E., Etruscan kings built his temple on Circum Maximus. On May 15, the day of his festival, Mercuria, merchants traditionally sprinkled water from Mercury's sacred well at Porta Capena in Italy on their heads, their wares, and their ships. Temples to Mercury or Hermes existed in many places, but his cult center was at Greek Arkadia, the place of his birth, where his festival was called Hermoea.

Hermes was born in a cave, and before the babe was a day old, he had stolen Apollo's cattle. While he was stealing the cattle, the clever young god made the first lyre from a tortoise shell, and he invented the flute. Not only did he steal but he also covered his tracks, and by doing so became the patron of thieves, pickpockets, and highway bandits. Endearing to rogues, liars, hucksters, and scoundrels, one of his appellations is Hermes Dolios ("the schemer").

The son of Zeus and Maia—goddess of clouds and one of the celestial Pleiades, the seven daughters of Atlas—Hermes, in earliest times, was a shamanic figure. One of his most important roles was that of *psychopompos* ("conductor of the soul") or taking the dead to Hades. Traveling between the world of mortals and the world of spirit, he was portrayed differently than the smooth-faced eternal youth (*puer aeternus*) we are accustomed to. There he was a bearded old man (*senex* messenger to the dead, "senile"). To the pre-Roman Etruscans he was Turms, who guided the deceased to the Underworld and also served as messenger of the gods; to Sumerians he was Gud; to Assyrians Nabu ("the herald"); and to the Egyptians Thoth. The Celts equated Mercury with Lugh of the many skills because of his versatility, and the Germans with Wodan.

In classical Greece images of Hermes were placed outside of Athenian houses for luck. These square or rectangular pillars of stone or bronze with a bust of his head at the top and male genitals at the base were called hermes ("pile of marker stones"), *hermai,* or herms and were used to mark roads and borders, thus associating the god with crossroads and boundaries. Statues of Mercury or Hermes guard gymnasia and stadia because he inventled wresting and boxing.

The swiftest planet bears the god's name, and the metal quicksilver, also called mercury, is sacred to him. The best day to call upon him or perform spells requiring his help is Wednesday (Wodan's day), in French, Mercredi, or Mercury's day.

This slick-talking, street savvy, swift-footed deity is right at home on any busy metropolitan street, in airports and train stations, and in cyberspace. As god of commerce and wealth, Mercury's statuette stands on the peak of New York's Grand Central Station. Charming Mercury delivers floral messages without delay and travels the highways in a car named for him. He lends his sharp wit to electronic communication, computers, and the Mercury Space Project. Regardless of which name we call him, Mercury thrives in our postmodern world.

See **Caduceus, Coinage and Currency, The** *Iliad,* **The** *Aenead,* **Cumaean Sybil, Nike, Oracles and Seers.**

83

The Muses

Anyone who has ever written a poem or painted a picture, anyone who has acted, sung, or played music, has known his or her muse. Writers complain their muse has deserted them. Others cultivate their relationships with their muse, sometimes seeing their personal muse in the form of a woman or women in their lives. The muse is one of the many gifts of the ancient Greeks to the world.

Originally there were three Muses among the Titans, those giants who preceded the later Olympians in the Greek pantheon. These first three Muses were daughters of the Earth Mother Gaia and the Sky Father Ouranos. Their names were Melete ("practice" or "meditation"), Mneme or Mnenmosyne ("memory"), and Aoide ("song"). Of these, Mnenmosyne is the best known, for she conceived, by Zeus, the nine goddesses of the arts and sciences we also know as the Muses.

The eldest, Calliope ("beautiful voice"), was goddess of epic poetry. Calliope was mother to Orpheus, the singer who saved Odysseus and his men from the Sirens' call. He also sought his dead wife, Eurydice, in

Hades. Calliope is depicted with stylus and wax tablets. The second sister, Clio ("proclaimer"), presides over the composition of heroic poetry and history. Images of her show her with a parchment scroll or set of tablets. Melpomene ("choir") is muse of tragedy. Melpomene is shown wearing *cothurnus*, the boots traditionally worn by tragic actors, and holding a tragic mask in one hand and a knife or a club in the other. The muse of music and lyric poetry is Euterpe ("heavenly," "rejoicing well," or "delight"), sometimes called "Giver of Pleasure." Euterpe invented the double-flute and is shown holding a flute. The fifth sister is Erato ("lovely"), muse of erotic poetry and hymns and of mimic imitation. She is depicted with a lyre. Terpsichore ("whirler" or "delight of dancing") presides over dance and dramatic chorus. The seductive but dangerous Sirens, who lured seafarers to their deaths, were Terpsichore's daughters—the Sirens, "whom rosey Terpsikhore brought forth by the stormy embraces of her bull-horned husband Akheloos" (Dionysiaca). She is portrayed sitting down holding a lyre and plectrum with which to pluck it. Urania ("queen of the mountains") rules astronomy and astrology. By the god Apollo, Urania is mother of Linus, the personification of the lamentation song, and Hymenaios, the personification of the wedding song, whence our word "hymen." She is pictured with a globe and staff. Thalia ("good cheer") is mistress of comedy and pastoral poetry. She is more rural than the other more cosmopolitan muses, and is depicted carrying a shepherd's crook and a comic mask. The youngest, Polyhymnia ("many songs"or "many praises"), inspires sacred song and eloquence. Unlike her sisters, Polyhymnia is not portrayed with any tools or symbols. Rather, she is shown as a serious young woman, in a pensive and meditative attitude. In some images, she is depicted dressed in a long cloak, her elbow resting on a pillar, and holding her finger in her mouth. Sappho of Lesbos was called the "tenth Muse" because of her inspired poetry and song.

Also known as the Ladies of Helicon for a grove and spring sacred to them on Mount Helicon, the Muses sang at the feasts, weddings, and funerals of gods and heroes. They were companions to Apollo, and they wandered with Dionysus and his worshippers. The Muses are the source of our words "music" and "museum"—the house of the Muses.

See **Sappho.**

84

Nike

Nike was not one of the Olympians, although she lived with the gods on Mount Olympus. Like Hekate and Dionysus, Nike was a much older deity whose mother, the Titan Styx, was goddess of the river in Hades, which all who would enter the Underworld must cross. Styx actually means "hateful/abhorrent." Nike's father was Pallas, the "warrior-youth," and her siblings were Power, Force, and Rivalry. Nike's name means "victory" in Greek, just as her Roman name, Victoria, means victory in Latin.

Nike is often seen in the company of the war goddess Athena, the undefeatable. The ancient bards—Hesiod, Homer, Aristophanes, Cicero, and others—sang of Nike, calling her "giver of sweetness" and "trim-ankled Nike." An Orphic hymn invokes her thusly:

> O powerful Nike, by men desired, with adverse breasts to dreadful fury fired, thee I invoke, whose might alone can quell contending rage and molestation fell. Correct? I don't know what it means. It means she can prevent, avoid or fight off molestation—molestation fell. 'Tis thine in battle to confer the crown, the victor's prize, the mark of sweet renown; for thou rulest all things, Nike divine! And glorious strife, and joyful shouts are thine. Come, mighty Goddess, and thy suppliant bless, with sparkling eyes, elated with success; may deeds illustrious thy protection claim, and find, led on by thee, immortal fame.

Ancient sculptors, too, honored Nike by carving her in marble, ivory, and gold and casting her statues in bronze. Depicted on vases, she carries a *kithara*, or lyre, and a *phiale*, or cup, or perhaps she is holding an incense burner and a flower *phiale*. Elsewhere she is shown pouring libations from a jug over an altar. Nike bestows the crown on victorious athletes in games of skill and strength and on returning warriors.

Nike, also known as Winged Victory, has had a remarkably diverse presence in contemporary culture. During the Cold War of the 1950s, the U.S. Army built arms they called Nike missiles, once again invoking her quality of granting victory in battle. A statue of winged Nike stands atop the state capitol building of Arizona. A manufacturer of athletic footwear calls itself Nike, and uses a highly stylized wing as its logo, thereby giving the athletes who wear their shoes a divine edge so that they may be victorious in competitions. Finally, her image appears on the well-known "Mercury dime" minted in the United States from 1916 to 1945. Although it is misnamed the Mercury dime, presumably because the figure wears a winged helmet, the image is that of the comely, swift-footed Nike.

85

Oracles and Seers

The notion that one can foretell the future, prophesy events, or divine esoteric meanings from various phenomena has always been connected with Pagans. Augury is the act of prophesying the future or soothsaying. The word "prophet" means "someone who speaks beforehand." Oracles are those believed to speak directly from the gods. The word "oracle" also refers to the location where they worked. Their messages were god given, in response to a request, plea, or petition. The proclamations of the oracle were often enigmatic and open to interpretation, and they sometimes were misinterpreted.

Some seers are born with second sight, given the gift by a god, or learned the skill from an adept. A famous example of the latter is the tragic Cassandra, who utters true prophecies but is cursed by the god Apollo, never to be believed. She warns the Trojans against the Greeks' gift of a horse. The blind seer Laocoon confirms her, to no avail. Another blind prophet was the Theban Tiresias, who lacked the ability to see but instead could understand the songs of birds, walk like those who can see with a magic cornel-wood staff, and retained his oracular ability even after death when he continued to prophesy in Hades.

Other oracles were connected with specific holy places. The Pythia at the temple of Apollo at Delphi on the slopes of Mount Parnassas, for example, presided at the most famous oracular site in the ancient world. People came from throughout the Mediterranean seeking her prophecy. The Pythia sat upon a tripod over a crack in the rocks that ran deep within the earth. Fumes emitting from the crack induced her into a prophetic state. The oldest and second most important oracle in ancient Greece was at Dodona, dedicated to the goddess Dione, the god Zeus, and the demi-god Heracles. This sanctuary was the site of a festival featuring athletic games, musical contests, and drama. A wall enclosed a holy oak, perhaps the manifestation of Dione. So powerful was the magic of the tree that a single timber from Dodona comprised part of Jason's ship, the Argos, and empowered the vessel itself with the gift of prophecy. The Greek oracle whose predictions were considered the most accurate was at the temple of Apollo on the island of Crete.

Beyond Greece, Alexander the Great consulted the oracle at the temple of the god Ammon in Egypt. The Cumaean Sybil presided over an oracle at Cumae near present-day Naples in Italy. The word "Sybil," derived from the Anatolian goddess Kybele, is a surname or title from the role performed. A deep cave at Cumae was said to be one of the gateways to Tartarus, the Underworld place of torment, and it is through this entry that the Sybil helps Aeneas enter the Underworld where he speaks with Tiresias.

In other mythologies, the heads of the revered dead offer a different kind of magical counsel. The ancient Welsh, for instance, consulted the head of their slain leader, Bran the Blessed, on all matters of importance, and he answered. In the Norse pantheon, Odin takes the severed head of the god Mimir to Asgard for consultation as an oracle. Today the pre-Christian Norse oracular practice called *seid* (also spelled *seidhr*) is experiencing a revival, as Pagans in Scandinavia, England, and North America sing the old magic songs to take the oracle into the otherworld. The seeress, called *seidkhona*, or seer, *seidmadhur*, speaks from the High Seat, a raven at her or his ear, while drums, chanting, and firelight help sustain the trance state.

See **Cumaean Sybil, Delphic Oracle, The *Aenead*.**

86

Pan

The Greek figure of Pan, god of woods, rocky crests, and wild animals, of pastures, shepherds, and flocks, appeals more to NeoPagans than any other male deity. Pan, whose name means "all" or "everything," with his uninhibited sexuality, and his love of the outdoors, personifies an elemental force of Nature. Typically, he has a wrinkled face with a prominent chin and two horns on his forehead, and a hairy body with the hindquarters and legs of a goat. He wears a lynx pelt and carries a reed pipe, a shepherd's crook, or a pine branch. Sometimes Pan is shown wearing a crown of pine needles and oftentimes he has an erect penis. Irish iconoclast Oscar Wilde, shortly before our time (1854–1900), recognized this appeal when he called for Pan's return:

> *O goat-foot God of Arcady!*
> *This modern world is grey and old,*
> *And what remains to us of thee?*

. . .

Then blow some trumpet loud and free,
And give thine oaten pipe away,
Ah, leave the hills of Arcady!
This modern world hath need of thee!

During the day Pan roams the hills slaying wild beasts. In the evenings he plays sweet and low on his pipes of reed, in the company of other retinue of the god Dionysus, singing nymphs, and Charites ("Graces"). Pan's parentage is unclear; some say he's the son of Hermes. All we really know, however, is that when the midwife at Pan's birth first saw his bearded face, she fled in fear, and it is from her disturbance that we get the word "panic," or irrational terrors.

The best-known story of Pan concerns his pursuit of a nymph named Syrinx. To escape his attentions, Syrinx runs until she reaches water's edge, where she cries to water nymphs for help and they turn her into marsh reeds that emit a plaintive melody when wind moves over them. Pan is left with nothing of Syrinx to embrace except the reeds. He joins together reeds of different sizes to create the instrument we call the syrinx, or Panpipes. Another nymph, named Pitys, escapes Pan's unwanted amorous attentions by being changed into a pine tree. Another object of Pan's limitless lust is the nymph Echo, who dances and sings and scorns the love of man. For this Pan tells his followers to kill her, which they do by dismembering her and spreading the pieces all over Earth. The only thing that remains of Echo is her voice, which repeats the last words of others.

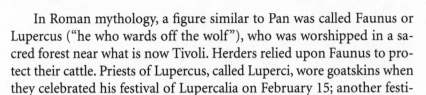

In Roman mythology, a figure similar to Pan was called Faunus or Lupercus ("he who wards off the wolf"), who was worshipped in a sacred forest near what is now Tivoli. Herders relied upon Faunus to protect their cattle. Priests of Lupercus, called Luperci, wore goatskins when they celebrated his festival of Lupercalia on February 15; another festival was held in honor of Faunus on December 5.

Puck is a western European cousin of Pan. Like Pan, Puck is pictured as having the body of a goat, the torso, arms, and head of a man, with horns on his head. And like Pan, Puck is a randy fellow much loved by NeoPagans. Puck enjoys a good time and often plays tricks in the moonlight, like leading travelers astray or blowing out candles. Unlike Pan, however, Puck was a *genius*, or place-spirit, connected to a specific area. Puck is called *puca* in Old English, *puki* ("devil") in Old Norse, *pwcca* in Welsh, and *pooka* in Irish. These terms for Puck lay in a layer of language deeper than Celtic and North Germanic languages. The word "puck" is used in Ireland to mean "goat." When Puck mixes with humans, he disguises himself as the man Robin Goodfellow.

Pan is a primary Horned God of NeoPaganism, and although they are antlered rather than horned, the Celtic Cernunnos and Herne the Hunter in Britain are equated with Pan.

See **Gundestrup Cauldron.**

VI

SACRED SITES

We've all experienced sacred sites, often when we're out enjoying one of Nature's wonders, but perhaps also when we enter a cave, a building such as a cathedral, or a grove of trees (called a neme-ton). Sacred sites are places where a sense of sacredness, or the presence of divinity, can be easily apprehended by many people. They are places people have congregated over a long period of time for devotion, celebration, consultation with an oracle, or a glimpse into the mysteries of life. One example from the natural world is the Hindu reverence for the sacred Ganges River, said to purify bathers of all negative karma, just as John the Baptist purified Christians in the River Jordan.

There are two types of sacred site—natural geological forma-tions/phenomena and human constructions. The former includes such places as forests, springs, caves, deserts, and mountaintops. The latter are temples, shrines, and other edifices made by people, often on the site of a sacred spring or where a *nemeton*, or sacred grove, had previously grown.

Pagans journey to these places when they go on personal vision quests seeking to overcome challenges and discover a view of their futures. They visit sacred sites seeking a more direct connection with the Mother, direct communication with Her, and for counsel and healing.

Some of the sacred sites in this section, such as the Parthenon in Athens and the city of Petra in modern-day Jordan, lie abandoned and in ruins. Sacred forests such as the legendary Broceliande in Brittany have been denuded of their trees. Sacred rivers and springs have been channeled into underground urban water systems or run under contemporary streets. Some sacred sites have been "developed" and are covered with buildings, paved thoroughfares, or parking lots. Some, such as mountaintops, volcanoes and distant deserts, are so remote and inaccessible by ordinary means they have remained pristine and inviolate. And some, like the strange faces found on what we call Easter Island, remain shrouded in mystery; we don't know who erected them, when, or for what purpose. We do know that they are Pagan.

87

Brugh na Boine

Brugh na Boine, also known as Newgrange, is a megalithic (giant stone) mound and earthwork complex in the Boyne valley of northeastern Ireland. The most famous part of this complex is the chambered tomb or ritual enclosure, built sometime between 3200 and 3700 B.C.E., making the buried chambers one of the oldest extant buildings in the world. Like Stonehenge, this structure was created to mark events of the solar and lunar cycles. At dawn during the Winter Solstice, beams of sunlight illuminate the main hallway and chamber, falling on designs carved into the stone at the back of the chamber. The nearby mound of Dowth reflects this celestial orientation in its illumination by the Winter Solstice sunset. Knowth, also a part of this megalithic complex, marks the sunrise at the Autumn Equinox. Together, these three sites form the largest known megalithic mound-complex astronomical calculator in Europe.

The great entrance stone at the Brugh is carved with a large triple spiral, along with diamond shapes and other spirals. As the sun rises on the Winter Solstice, the light moves up the exterior surface of the stone, finally rising above it and entering a small light box above the main entrance to the Brugh. The light takes six minutes to crawl along the floor until it begins to climb the end stone at the back of the chamber. Moonlight also enters the chamber at different intervals over a repeating 18.6-year period. One kerbstone (paving stone forming part of a curb) at Knowth has carvings on it that can be interpreted as an explicit mapping of the moon's waxing and waning and a lunar calendrical year. Taken together, the Knowth, Newgrange, and Dowth complex mark solar events for an eightfold solar/lunar cycle of the year.

Three other kerbstones are found along the outside of the chamber within Newgrange; they are also carved with symbols, hidden now on their inner surfaces. Each of these three stones marks significant solar and lunar events during the course of the year by the passage of light and shadow over the stones. Two of these stones are aligned with standing stones that mark sunrise on May 6 and August 8, about the times when Pagans now celebrate Beltain and Lughnassadh.

In the Irish literary tradition, the Brugh na Boine, the Hostel on the Boyne River, was said to be the home of the Daghda Mór (Dagda), the "good god" with a hearty appetite, who is one of the main deities of the Tuatha de Danann or Children of the Goddess Danu. At one point, the Dagda's son, Oengus Mac Óg (Angus), asks the Dagda for a Brugh of his own. The Dagda replies that he has no Brugh for Angus.

"Let me stay a day and a night in your own Brugh," Angus asks. The Daghda complies, but when he returns and asks Angus to leave, Angus replies to him, "It is in days and nights that all time is measured, and so you have given me this place for all time and eternity." This is an example of the magical power of a riddle, one of the most highly respected virtues among the Celts. This one day and night requested and granted is symbolic of *every* day and night, and therefore Angus claims ownership in that symbolic time—all time and eternity. Because of the riddling nature of the request and the claim, the Dagda can't argue that it's not true.

In the cycle of days and nights, we measure our lives, and the passage of all time. The Brugh na Boine is a potent reminder of the passage of these eternal cycles.

See **May Day, Cerne Abbas Giant.**

88

Carnac

The megalithic site at Carnac, in Brittany, France, is made of more than three thousand standing stones, dolmens, or stone arches, and tumuli (burial mounds). Megalith literally means giant stone. Many dolmens and tumuli were used as burial sites by the Neolithic and later Bronze

Age cultures (eighth to fourth millennia B.C.E.) that erected them. Tumuli are also known as barrow mounds.

Carnac consists of massive avenues of stone and dolmen arches. The placement and erection of these megaliths are an extremely impressive feat of social cooperation and Neolithic engineering. These stones were laid by our Pagan ancestors more than five thousand years ago, by a civilization that would have needed to have an abundance of food and resources so that the people could devote themselves to the cutting, transportation, and erection of the stones. If there had not been enough resources, the people would instead have had to remain occupied with farming, gathering, fishing, and hunting simply to survive. The builders also would have had to have a belief in the importance of undertaking such a difficult and consuming project.

Such massive earthworks are often thought to have been created for religious purposes. We cannot prove this today, but the experience of a visit to the site can convince any NeoPagan, or anyone else, that this place is indeed sacred. Some megalithic structures, like Stonehenge, on Salisbury Plain in England, were apparently giant astronomical calculators, tracing the movements of the sun, the moon, and the stars, and able to predict with great accuracy the occurrences of solar and lunar eclipses and the turning of the seasons.

In medieval Ireland, Scotland, and Wales, these megalithic structures were often the focus of pilgrimages by people desiring dreams or visions. They were sometimes seen as the homes of deities; Brugh na Boine, home of Angus, is a good example. It was believed that to sleep on a barrow mound was a magical, though highly dangerous, activity—one would have a vision, go mad, or die as a result of this ritual of dream seeking. In many places, megalithic monuments such as those found at Carnac are still regarded as magical or sacred places associated with land spirits, elves, the Sídhe, or the spirits of the ancestors—this last no doubt because many of them are places of burial. Other examples are Massleberg in southern Sweden (one of about a dozen in that country); the Dolmen de Ageltus, also known as Dolmen ex Axeitos, in Galicia (named for a local Celtic tribe), Spain (among eight in that region alone); and Druidenstein and Frauenbillkreug in Germany. (There are more than thirty extant megalithic sites in Germany; many others have been destroyed and their stones used in paving.) Sites in the Western Hemisphere include a four-thousand-year-old megalith north of Boston, Massachusetts, Balanced Rock in North Salem, New York; and a dolmen said to be two to ten thousand years old in southern Brazil. Beyond Europe and the Americas, megaliths are found as far dispersed as Africa and India. NeoPagans continue this tradition, at Carnac and other powerful places.

See **Brugh na Boine.**

89

Cerne Abbas Giant

The giant of Cerne Abbas, also called the Rude Giant, located about seven miles north of Dorchester in Dorset, England, is a massive male figure believed to be a Dagda-like god carved into the chalk of a grassy hillside. This 200-foot-tall giant carries a 167-foot-long club. He has a detailed face, nipples, ribs, and a 30-foot-long erect phallus. Ancient, its age unknown, but believed to date from the second millennium B.C.E., the figure has been there since long before the Celtic peoples arrived in Britain.

One contention is that the image represents the god Helith, or Hercules, cut there in the second century C.E. by colonialist subjects of the Roman emperor Commodius, who was believed to be Hercules incarnate.

This figure may have been the representation of a fertility god of the early inhabitants of Britain. Club and phallus are both icons of masculine fertility. In differing versions of tales about the Irish god Dagda, it is said that he has a club that he drags behind him, which leaves great furrows in the earth. In other, less edited versions of these tales, it's the Dagda's phallus that digs the ditches. The Dagda himself is said to be the father of many of the Tuatha de Danann, the deities of Ireland. While the Dagda is from a culture that developed long after the Cerne Abbas Giant was carved, stories of gods like this may have been part of the spark behind these stories.

The use of phallic images in fertility magic has an ancient and honorable history. Its pull is still strong, and found in many cultures. We know that May Day festivities were celebrated in the vicinity of the giant from the writings of Philip Stubbs, when, in 1853, he wrote, "Hundreds of men, women, and children go off to the woods and groves and spend all the night in pastimes, and in the morning return with birch boughs and branches of trees to deck their assembles withal." Even today, women who want to become pregnant sometimes go to the Giant to lie on the grass of its phallus as an act of sympathetic magic.

Fertility gods in many mythologies are the force behind the creation of the world. In some cultures, ithyphallic gods created the world without the aid of a mother, simply by shedding their seed. Other ithyphallic gods are the Greek Hermes and Pan, Osiris in Egypt, and Shiva in India. These gods are usually represented as a bull, ram, phallus, or other similar symbols of their life-giving force. This male force of creativity is often celebrated today by gay men in the NeoPagan movement, such as the Witches of the Faggot Tradition, seeking positive images of male power not linked to the oppression of women. Such positive images of male power are a thing we can all celebrate.

A spring rises at the foot of the hill upon which the giant is carved. In ancient times the water was known as the "silver well," but was called St. Augustine's Well after the arrival of Christianity in the region. The spring provides a wonderful feminine complement to the powerful masculine giant above.

See **Bridget, Isis and Osiris, May Day, Mercury/Hermes, Pan, Stonehenge.**

90

Delphic Oracle

The Oracle at the temple of Apollo at Delphi on the slopes of Mount Parnassus in Greece is perhaps the most famous oracular site in the world, even today. In its day, which lasted many centuries, people came from throughout the Mediterranean seeking the advice of the Pythia, for so its priestess was called. Today it lies in abandoned ruins.

The peculiar attributes of the site were accidentally discovered by goats. When they wandered near a chasm, they made strange sounds and leaped about in a state of possession. Then, when a goatherd approached the chasm to investigate, he too became possessed and began to prophesy. For this reason, goats were the traditional sacrifice to the oracle. Word of this marvel, considered a divine gift from Gaia (Mother Earth) herself, spread, and more and more people were drawn to the site. Some, unable to control the frenzy brought on by the fumes, leapt to their deaths in the chasm, so the people in the region decided it was best to appoint a single prophetess.

The seat of the oracle was in a cave hollowed deep in the earth, where the breath that inspired divine frenzy issued from a small opening. A three-legged stool, called a tripod, was contrived to straddle the opening and give the Pythia a safe place to sit and gain her inspiration. Young virgins, because of their purity and innocence, served as the first oracles, but in time sexual violence was visited upon the prophetess, so maidens no longer served and instead an elderly woman presided. The Pythia was consulted on all major undertakings—wars, alliances, the founding of colonies, and such—and thus exerted considerable influence on the affairs of state.

In one version of the origin of the oracle, Cretan sailors were said to have been the first priests at the Delphic sanctuary, led there by Apollo himself in the form of a dolphin, from whence the name Delphi. The first of several temples erected at Delphi was made of laurel brought from Tempe. A second temple was made by bees from beeswax and feathers. The third bronze temple was said to have either been swallowed in a chasm in the earth or melted by fire.

In time, two princes had a stone temple erected, which was later accompanied by sanctuaries and palaces. Singers and composers came to Delphi to compete for prizes for the best hymn to the god Apollo. The winner was crowned with a laurel wreath. Thamyris, who won the third contest, loved the youth Hyacinthus, so was considered the first man to fall in love with males.

Delphi was considered to be the center of the universe. This was represented by a carved stone omphalos (navel), "where Phoebus ['bright sun,' another name for Apollo] has at earth's navel his prophetic seat" (spoken by Hermes in the writings of Euripides). There are three maxims engraved upon a column at Delphi by order of the Seven Sages: (a) "Know yourself," (b) "Nothing in excess," and (c) "A pledge, and ruin is near." Because it was considered to be the center of the universe, many riches and spoils of war were deposited in the treasure houses at Delphi.

Delphi is a site of pilgrimage for NeoPagans. There, amid the ruins of the temples and sanctuaries, geologists have found the geothermal emissions coming from a chasm directly under Apollo's temple.

See **Oracles and Seers.**

91

Emain Macha

Emain Macha, also known as Navan Fort, is a Celtic hill fort in Ulster named for the Irish horse-goddess Macha. One notable structure on this site was an immense round house built between the seventh and fourth centuries B.C.E. It had five concentric rings of oak poles covered with thatch and was rebuilt five times over the course of its five hundred to a thousand years' existence.

Macha has three faces: seer, warrior, and sovereignty. There are three stories about Macha and the origins of Emain Macha. This is one of them.

At Emain Macha, so this story goes, there was a widowed man with motherless children. One day while he was gone, a woman came to his house, cleaned the entire house, washed and fed the children, and put them to bed. Then she went sunwise around his home, invoking prosperity for him. She had a delicious hot meal waiting for him when he returned in the evening. On the condition that he never speak of her or utter her name outside the house she agreed to marry him. He agreed to her conditions, for she would leave him if he didn't. Eventually the woman, who was in fact the goddess Macha, became pregnant. When Macha was near her term and ready to give birth, her husband went to the king of Ulster's assembly at the great round house for one of the four high festivals of the year. There was horse racing, and the man, emboldened by drink, boasted before the king that he had a wife at home who could outrun any of the king's horses.

The king, angry at this outrageous claim, demanded that Macha be brought before him and made to race. Macha, suffering the pains of labor, begged to be allowed at least to give birth first, but the king would not relent. To save her husband's honor, she raced against the horses. Macha, a goddess, was swifter than all the horses, even in labor, but at the end of the race she fell to the ground and gave birth to twins (*emain*), and so the site is named Emain Macha, the Twins of Macha.

As Macha gave birth, she uttered a curse against the Ulstermen: She said that in the hour of their greatest need, they would suffer the pangs of birth for four days and five nights, lying helpless against their enemies as a woman in childbed. Only the women, the smallest boys and the oldest men unable to fight, and the hero Cu Chuliann would be spared. After this, Macha turned and left, never seeing her husband again. The curse was for seven times seven generations. It was this that nearly led to Ulster's defeat in the epic tale of the Tain Bo Cualigne (the Cattle Raid of Cooley).

The story of Macha teaches the importance of keeping one's promises, as Macha's husband had promised not to speak of her. It tells us that anyone we meet may be a deity in disguise, so we must treat them with respect. It gives a model of women's strength, endurance, and power, as Macha raced the king's horses and triumphed despite her labor pains. It also shows the consequences of cruelty and unreasonable demands, which created the conditions for the defeat in one of the greatest tales of the Irish literary tradition. Even today, we can explore stories like this for the lessons they teach for our daily lives. The plain upon which this famous race took place remains a place of pilgrimage today.

92

Hill of Tara

Perhaps no other ancient Celtic site stirs more sentiment in the hearts of the Irish diaspora than the Hill of Tara. Tara (*Teanair* in Gaelic) is a long, low limestone ridge in County Meath, Leinster, Ireland, not far from the River Boyne (river of the bovine goddess Boann). The remains of about thirty earthwork monuments are visible from the summit. The earliest monument was built between 3030 and 2190 B.C.E. according to radiocarbon dating. The majority of the monuments, however, were built during the fourth and third millennia B.C.E. Among them are the

Mound of the Hostages, a small passage grave dating from 2000 B.C.E. There is also a ringfort with three banks known as the Rath of the Synods. A bank and a ditch called the Royal Enclosure surrounds two linked ringforts known as the Royal Seat and the Forradh. The Forradh (elevated mound) is surrounded by two banks and two ditches. An enormous stone penis called the Lia Fáil, the "Stone of Destiny" or "Stone of Knowledge," stands in the center of the Forradh. The Lia Fáil stone cries out under the destined king, uttering a screech for all to hear. Another way the stones confirmed the kingship was when two flagstones called Blocc and Bluegne accepted a man, they would open before him until his chariot passed between them. At all other times but for that moment they stood so close together that only a hand could pass sideways between them.

Ireland, Eire, the land itself is goddess. The man who would be king must be the embodiment of the masculine principle. As an acknowledgment of a man's entitlement to the kingship, at the coronation banquet a stallion representing the king ritually mated with a mare representing the goddess herself.

In the times when Tara, in Meath ("middle"), served as a place of court and council, the four provincial halls were arranged around the Central Hall—Munster in the south, Connaught in the west, Ulster in the north, and Leinster in the east. At their banquets, when all the kings/chieftains, *aes dána* (people of art), *bo-áire* (cattle-owning warrior nobility), free non-nobles, charioteers, druids, *fili* (poets), *brehons* (lawyers), doctors/healers, historians, musicians, fools/jesters, *seanchai* (storytellers), harpers, commoners, and slaves (yes, unfortunately, the Irish, too, had slaves) had gathered, the seating arrangement was the same. The Gaelic terms for the four directions—north, south, east, west—also meant left, right, before, behind, respectively. Most NeoPagan rites are performed from within the center of a circle marked by the four cardinal directions.

Such is the influence of Tara as a center of religious and political import that in the early nineteenth century Irish Member of Parliament Daniel O'Connell hosted one million Irish at a peaceful rally for Home Rule there. Whatever the mysteries clothed in the emerald grass on the hill of Tara, this ancient Pagan sacred site continues to seduce all who would open to her magic.

93

Labyrinths

A labyrinth is a term for a unicursal (one line) design of a particular circular shape. Most labyrinths have seven levels or circuits from the outside to the inside. This style is called a classical labyrinth. It, as well as other styles of labyrinths and mazes, are found constructed in many media—stone, turf, paint, basketry—and occurring all over the world from all times. The oldest examples are simple, and have been found in Europe as far north as the polar regions, and in India and Java in the east. The same and similar designs were used by Native Americans in pre-Columbian New Mexico and Arizona. More recent examples are found in Syria, China, Peru, Ireland, Australia, and Nepal.

Petroglyphs (carvings in stone) from three thousand years ago are the oldest known labyrinth designs. However, the Meander Pattern, or Greek Key, design, which is a simpler form of labyrinth pattern, has been found inscribed on figurines from the Ukraine from 15,000 to 18,000 B.C.E. The oldest positively dated labyrinth pattern was inscribed on a clay tablet in the palace of King Nestor in Pylos, southern Greece, around 1230 B.C.E. A generation earlier Nestor dispatched ships from Pylos to aid Agamemnon in the siege of Troy.

There are other connections between labyrinths and Troy. Troy was said to have seven walls. The wall of Troy pattern in Greek art mimics the design of the labyrinth. Welsh shepherd boys cut seven-layered labyrinth patterns, said to represent Troy's seven walls, into turf. They called these figures *Caerdroia*, meaning either City of Troy or City of Turnings. A town in Sweden, where there is a stone classical-style labyrinth, is called *Trojeborg*, which means Trojan fort. Scandinavian labyrinths are generally found in coastal areas, where they are thought to have been constructed to trap malevolent trolls to ensure safe fishing expeditions.

Another design sometimes, inaccurately, called a labyrinth is the maze. Mazes differ from labyrinths in that they are a puzzle involving choices, blocks, and dead ends, whereas a unicursal labyrinth has only one path to the center and out again. The medieval style of labyrinth, more complicated than the classical, is divided into four quadrants, each with seven sharp turns. The labyrinth at Chartres Cathedral in France is an example of this pattern, as is the one at Grace Cathedral in San Francisco.

The word "labrys" is Greek for "double axe." The labrys is the symbol for the Minoan dynasty of ancient Crete, site of the most famous labyrinth at the city of Knossos. The Minoan labyrinth, technically a maze, was designed by the Greek architect Daedalus at the behest of King Minos, to hold his half-human, half-bull son, the Minotaur. Each year seven youths and seven maidens from Greece were sacrificed to the monster. The hero Theseus was sent on a mission to slay the Minotaur, but Ariadne, daughter of Minos and his wife Pasiphae and sister to the monster, became enamored of Theseus, so she gave him the secret of how to get out of the maze once he'd gone in and slain the Minotaur. This secret was a ball of yarn. Although no site in Crete has been identified as the labyrinth that held the Minotaur, Cretan coins from 300 to 100 B.C.E. are stamped with the labyrinth design.

There is renewed interest today in labyrinths among Pagans as well as people of other religions. Labyrinth designs can be found on public land and private, indoors and outdoors, in tile, pavement, rock, turf, or painted, even on cloth. There are small handheld labyrinths for meditation, labyrinths painted on canvas for temporary use, and glorious garden labyrinths.

94

The Parthenon

The Parthenon is reputed to be the most perfect Doric temple ever built, one of the most widely recognized symbols of Hellenic cultural achievement. The temple site has seen continuous human occupation since at least 2800 B.C.E. During the Mycenean period (1600–1100 B.C.E.) the hill where the temple sits was surrounded by a massive wall that protected the palace-temple of the Mycenean priest-kings. By the sixth century B.C.E. there were two temples to Athena (called Minerva by the Romans), probably built over older shrines. The present temple was dedicated to her when construction began in 439 B.C.E. The name itself, Parthenon, comes from the goddess Athena Parthenon—the Virgin Athena. She represents the highest order of spiritual development and the gifts of intellect and understanding. Pure in body, mind, and heart, Athena symbolizes the universal human aspiration for wisdom.

Architecture scholar Vincent Scully claims that "all Greek architecture explores and praises the character of a god or group of gods in a specific place. That place is itself holy and, before the temple was built upon it, embodied the whole of the deity as a recognized natural force." The Parthenon's precise topographical location, its astronomical orientation, and the sacred geometry that informed its proportions infuse the entire temple.

The temple was designed by two architects named Ictinus and Callicrates, under the supervision of the sculptor Phidias, with the encouragement of the powerful Athenian politician Pericles. It was constructed entirely of brilliant white marble, except for the roof tiles; the rectangular structure is more than 100 feet wide and over 230 feet long, and surrounded on all four sides by forty-six Doric columns. The original Parthenon contained three sets of sculptures: the pediments, the metopes, and the frieze. The latter two were part of the structure itself. The freestanding pediment statues at either end of the temple showed the birth of Athena from the head of Zeus at the east pediment and the struggle between Athena and Poseidon for Attica on the west.

The ninety-two metopes were individual statues in high relief on the outside of the building, in sets of thirty-two on each side and fourteen on each end. The metopes on the north depicted scenes from the Trojan War; those on the south showed the battle between the Greeks and the lapiths and centaurs; on the east, the gods fighting the giants; and on the west, battle between the Greeks and the Amazons.

The frieze was one long low-relief sculpture inside the building showing a procession. The friezes and pediment statues survive today, some broken and others intact, and are the subject of heated international litigation. The Greek government seeks their return from the British Museum and the Louvre.

The larger of the two interior rooms housed a glorious statue of Athena, fully armed with spear, helmet, and aegis. Made of wood, ivory, and gold by Phidias, the same artist who created the statue of Zeus in his temple at Olympus, the statue stood forty feet tall. Imagine the awe with which worshippers approached their goddess.

The goddess suffered the insult of having her gold removed by the tyrant Lachares to pay his army in 296 B.C.E. In the fifth century C.E. the temple was converted into a Christian church; in 1460 it housed a Turkish mosque; and in 1687 the inside was severely damaged by exploding gunpowder when the Venetian general Morosini bombarded the temple. Today automobile exhaust, industrial pollution, and acid rain are rapidly destroying the few remaining sculptures.

Despite all this, the Parthenon remains a place of beauty, and its goddess still has many worshippers worldwide. In 1982, the city of Nashville, Tennessee, erected an exact full-scale replica of the Parthenon. It, too, houses an enormous statue of Athena. Both of these temples are pilgrimage sites.

See **Nike, Dionysus, Olympic Games.**

95

Petra

Petra, described by the English romantic poet Lord Byron as "a rose-red city, half as old as time," was built by a nomadic tribe of Nabataean Arabs, around the sixth century B.C.E. Carved from dry rock, the city lies on the edges of the mountainous desert of the Wada Araba in Jordan, 155 miles southwest of modern Amman. Two miles square, the city is invisible in the mountains and contains extensive steps, water runlets, aqueducts, and reservoirs, as well as about a thousand temples. It sat at the crossroad of two major ancient trade routes where caravans carrying incense and other precious goods connected it to the Mediterranean, Egypt, and Mesopotamia. Artifacts such as terra cotta figures, ceramic jugs, storage jars, oil lamps, winged bronze statuettes, Nabataean coins, and scrolls found in Petra attest to its former wealth.

The approach to the city is called the Siq. Past small Nabataean tombs carved out of dry rock, a dusty trail twists and turns through a narrow passage with high stone walls on either side. The walls of the Siq are lined with channels (originally fitted with clay pipes) to carry drinking water into the city. Inside, a dam diverted an adjoining stream through a tunnel to prevent flooding. Through a cleft in the rock, one glimpses a pale reddish sandstone temple, carved with ornate pillars and portico. This building is called the Khazneh, meaning treasury, though it more likely was a temple or tomb.

The center of Petra is a wide paved street lined with columned buildings, with an amphitheater seating eight thousand, and a *nymphaeum* (public fountain) at one end—an open marketplace—and at the opposite end, the Temenos Gateway leads to the courtyard of the Temple of Dushara. The popular name for this temple is Qasr al-Bint Firaun ("the Castle of the Pharaoh's Daughter").

Dushara is a sun god and was the principal god of the Nabataeans. His mother and consort was the great mother goddess of Arabia—Allat. Some say his consort was Atargatis, a vegetation goddess of generation and fertility, or perhaps he had several lovers. Dushara could not be represented by an idol, only as an abstract symbol. He was represented by a tall four-cornered monolith, usually of rough-cut black stone, similar to an obelisk. One of these holy stones stands atop a plateau at Petra; they were also placed along roadways, in temples and shrines, and near graves. It was the practice of worshippers to kiss the stones, a custom continued today in other Arab religions.

Facing Dushara's temple is the Temple of the Winged Lion where Atargatis was worshipped. Atargatis is often depicted as fish-tailed, a mermaid, associated with moisture. As a vegetation goddess of generation and fertility, she protects her cities, as a moist sky goddess in cloud-like veil with eagles around her head.

A long, steep stairs lead up to the High Place of Sacrifice, where drainage channels have been cut into the rock to allow the blood of sacrificial animals to flow away. The Royal Tombs are three large structures carved in a rock face called King's Wall. There are other tombs of all sizes, including the Palace Tomb built in imitation of a Roman palace.

The mysterious Petra, with its walls of whorls and waves of color ranging from pale yellow, rich reds, and darker brown in the rock face, remains a glorious testament of our Pagan past "as old as time."

96

The Great Sphinx

This mysterious sculpture, a lion with a man's head, sits on the Giza plateau about six miles west of Cairo. Giza is the site of many other ancient archaeological treasures including the three large pyramids—the Great Pyramid of Cheops, the Pyramid of Chephren, and the Pyramid of Menkaura—as well as smaller Queens' pyramids, numerous rectan-

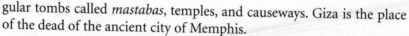

gular tombs called *mastabas*, temples, and causeways. Giza is the place of the dead of the ancient city of Memphis.

The Great Sphinx itself is carved from relatively soft limestone and extends to 241 feet in length and rises 65 feet in height. Each paw extends 56 feet from the body and the face is 13 feet wide. Much of the Sphinx has been eroded or desecrated: the nose was deliberately broken off. Fragments of the beard survive in museums. It once wore a *uraeus*, the royal rearing cobra headpiece that protects its wearer from evil, but this is long gone as well. The Sphinx wears the remains of the royal *nemes* (striped headcloth), which in ancient times was painted yellow and blue with the face painted red.

Theories about the date of its creation differ. The majority view is that it was built about 2540 B.C.E., at the same time as the Pyramid of Chephren nearby. But recent evidence of water erosion has led to another theory. About ten thousand years ago the region was wet and rainy, not arid like it is today. The belief is that in order for the Sphinx to have suffered water erosion, it would had to have been built between seven and ten thousand years ago, making it the oldest surviving structure from an ancient civilization.

The statue's meaning and the people who built it are unknown. In a reference from 1500 B.C.E. the Sphinx is referred to as Hor-em-akth, "Horus of the Horizon" and Bw-How, "Place of Horus." Horus is a falcon-headed god who is an aspect of the sun god, not the same image as a sphinx. The statue faces due east, toward the rising sun. We know that the ancient Egyptians worshipped the sun, and that they worshipped the Sphinx itself as the sun.

There are so many different sphinxes in Egypt that they have their own classification. A *crisosphinx* has the body of a lion and the head of a ram. The *hierocosphinx* also has a lion's body but the head is that of a hawk head. The Great Sphinx is of a type called an *androsphinx*, one with a lion body and a human head. Sphinxes often guard temple entrances. Rows of sphinxes stand at Luxor and Karnak, and twenty-six sphinxes have been discovered during the underwater dig at Alexandria in what is believed to be the Pharos Lighthouse.

The Greek sphinx, as opposed to the Egyptain ones, is a monster, a demon of death and destruction. She—for the Greek sphinx was female—was depicted as a winged lion with a woman's head, or a female with the breast, paws, and claws of a lion, a snake tail, and bird wings. Two beardless and wingless alabaster sphinxes found at Nineveh, capital of the Assyrian Empire in what is now Iraq, guarded palaces and temples. Other sphinxes were bearded men with quadruped bodies and wings. Ancient Phoenicians and Syrians also had sphinxes.

The enigmatic Great Sphinx speaks of a time and place lost to human memory. Replicas of sphinxes adorn many NeoPagan altars. Ask a Kemetic Pagan the meaning of the sphinx.

See **Seven Wonders of the Ancient World.**

97

Stonehenge

Stonehenge, on Salisbury Plain in Wiltshire, England, is one of the most famous Neolithic stone monuments in the world. Almost five thousand years old, it was built in three phases. Many of the stones were brought from sites in Wales, some of them originating over 240 miles from where Stonehenge stands. This is an incredible feat of engineering and transportation technology. This marvel was raised with nothing more than tools of stone, wood, leather, rope, and timber.

The site itself was in use as a temple or shrine for over seventeen hundred years. The stones are aligned to allow those with the knowledge of the skies to calculate the dates of solstices and equinoxes, and also to allow the prediction of solar and lunar eclipses. The use of Stonehenge as an astronomical calculator demonstrates a deep knowledge of astronomy and mathematics in the Neolithic era. It is sited in a place where the extreme northern and southern settings at the solstices of the sun are at right angles to each other, which is not the case even a few miles to the north or south of the circle. The knowledge required for such precision in setting is extremely sophisticated. Midsummer's dawn is marked by the rise of the sun over the Heel Stone, a thirty-five-ton monolith set at a distance from the main circle, and framed by a set of trilithons made of sandstone. Each of these stones weighs between twenty-five and fifty tons.

Long associated in the public imagination with Druids, this holy site originated over two thousand years before the Hallstadt culture that marks the origins of the Celts—about 1200 years B.C.E. Nevertheless, whether or not the Druids of old used Stonehenge as a temple, it is held sacred today by Druids and other Pagans all over the western world. In recent years, visitors to the site have painted graffiti on stones, chipped pieces from them, started fires on or near them, and otherwise caused serious damage. Because of this callous disregard, the English Heritage Society closed the site to the public entirely. Until only a few years ago, even at Midsummer's dawn the site was not open. Because of the efforts of British Druids, Stonehenge is once again available for ritual, but attendance requires an invitation.

Stonehenge has inspired replicas such as one in Oregon, but so far nothing compares to the engineering of our Pagan ancestors. Sites like Stonehenge, despite their seeming immortality, are much more easily damaged than most people realize. It can be difficult to imagine a site like this being destroyed by carelessness, but it is essential to remember that when visiting sacred sites, or any other place of ancient, natural beauty, it is our responsibility to care for these places so that future generations can revere and enjoy them in ages to come. Carrying out our rubbish, acting responsibly, leaving stones and other items intact, and leaving the sites untouched are an important part of maintaining such ancient holy sites. We must each act with care and in a spirit of reverence when we stand upon sacred land.

98

The Temple of Sekhmet

NeoPagans rarely have any kind of temples. We live in a much more multicultural world than most of our Pagan ancestors did. We share our world with people of all faith traditions. We in the United States have no god-kings or military or government that dictates whom we worship—and thank all the gods for that! We do, however, have a tendency to erect shrines and altars everywhere—in hotel rooms where we're staying, in our homes and backyards, in urban outdoor settings, on beaches, in woods, by streams—just about anywhere we feel a presence we want to honor.

But here in the United States we do have a few temples. One such is the Temple of Sekhmet, the ancient Egyptian lion-headed goddess called by thousands of names, over the ages, including "Lady of the Place of the Beginning of Time" and "the One Who Was Before the Gods Were." Sekhmet has found another home in another desert on another continent half a world away from her homeland. In 1992, Genevieve Vaughn and her daughters and friends built a straw bale, stuccoed, buff-colored temple in Cactus Springs, in the desert north of Las Vegas, Nevada. The structure houses a black human-sized statue of a seated Sekhmet sculpted by Marsha Gomez. Four arched doorways open the temple to the four winds and the open roof has a dome of seven interlocking copper rings. Maintained by Crone Priestess Patricia Pearlman, Sekhmet's temple is always open to visitors, pilgrims, and worshippers.

Sekhmet is also known as the Lady of Pestilence and the Greatest of Healers. Like the lioness, Sekhmet is the Goddess of Wrath and Destruction, and the Powerful Protectress of Her Children. She is a fiery goddess who enjoys the desert heat. As a healing goddess, Sekhmet heals when all other efforts have failed, for the methods she requires, like amputation or chemotherapy, are radical.

Sekhmet's Nevada temple sits on twenty acres of land near a nuclear test site. There are no buildings or other signs of human intrusion for miles, except the road and the discretely located home of the temple caretakers. There are, however, two trailers where women can visit overnight, and limited camping is allowed, again, for women only, although all are welcome to visit the temple. This land was once the home of the Western Shoshone and the land upon which the temple stands has been returned to the tribe. Nearby Western Shoshone, NeoPagans, and other environmental activists regularly work to eliminate nuclear weapons. As a desert-loving goddess of Justice and Retribution, Sekhmet and her temple offer a place of calm and refuge to them, and to all who come.

99

Tien Hao Temple

The oldest temple dedicated to a goddess in the United States is in San Francisco's Chinatown. Devoted to Tien Hao, the Queen of Heaven and Goddess of the Sea in ancient China, the temple was originally built in 1852, just at the end of the Gold Rush. At that time thousands of mostly illiterate and uneducated Chinese workers came to California to work in the mines, and later on the transcontinental railroad. The founding of the temple is attributed to the activity of the Chinese Sze Yap Company, one of the Six Companies of Chinatown. The early worshippers who came to Tien Hao for solace and guidance were mostly men, separated by an ocean from their loved ones and their culture. These men lived hard lives in a strange and inhospitable environment, but they found comfort in the presence of the goddess.

The temple is on the top floor of an unassuming building in an alley called Waverly Place. Leaving the bustle of activity in Chinatown, pilgrims climb three long flights of stairs, pass two mah jong parlors, and finally arrive at the entrance to another world. Here, the visitor is enveloped in the smell of incense and a pervading sense of serenity. The temple room is surrounded with beautifully ornamented gilded altars supporting statues of gods and goddesses. Some of the gods hold swords designed for fighting in the afterlife. Above, a profusion of red paper lanterns inscribed with the names of ancestors is suspended from the ceiling. At the far end of the temple is an altar with a statue of Tien Hao. She wears an elaborate headdress and is flanked by two fierce guardian figures.

Usually a temple attendant sits quietly near the entrance, unobtrusive but most willing to answer questions. This is a place to pay respects to one's ancestors and to the higher power of one's choice. The pilgrim is invited to light sticks of incense and pray and ask for good fortune

For many years it was the custom, on the weekend of Chinese New Year in February, for local San Francisco Bay Area Witches to pay their respects to Tien Hao at the temple and then brunch in Chinatown, all in memory of Grandma Julie Tower, founder of the "famtrad" (family tradition), called the Tower Family Tradition of American Witchcraft. The temple is open during the daytime, a peaceful haven for Chinese worshippers of Tien Hao and respectful visitors of all faith traditions.

100

Holy Waters

We Witches have a chant that goes: "The ocean is the beginning of the Earth. The ocean is the beginning of the Earth. All life comes from the sea. All life comes from the sea." And it does. Ninety-five percent of all life is in the oceans of the world. The womb waters where we all begin are like the salt water of the ocean, full of nutrients, creating a safe place for us to grow until we are ready to breathe air and live on land.

As far back as ancient Egypt, we see that the sun god Atum (Re) reposed in the primordial ocean (Nun). The first gods in Assyro-Babylonian myth arose from the coming together of sweet water (Apsu) and salt water (Tiamat). Surrounded by seas, the mythology of the seafaring Greeks is filled with sea goddesses, nymphs, and monsters. We get our word "dolphin" from the sea god Delphinos. Oceanus was the Titan of the sea. The Olympic god Poseidon, called Neptune by the Romans, rode white steeds that were the roaring waves, or rode in a seashell chariot pulled by seahorses. Aphrodite was foam-born. The Yoruba people of West Africa, and later the African diaspora in the Americas and the Caribbean, worship Yemaya, a goddess who loved mirrors and pearls and appears dressed in blue skirts with white ruffled underskirts, suggesting the waves meeting the shore.

Many peoples are fed by the oceans and rivers. For instance, the one-eyed goddess Sedna lives at the bottom of the ocean with the fishes and the seals. If she is not propitiated, she will not provide food for the Alaskan people.

Not only seawater but fresh water is sacred. Around the world people see the magic of rivers, lakes, ponds, streams, and waterfalls. Our Pagan ancestors saw the feminine divine in rivers. For example, the Boyne in Ireland is the river of the cow goddess Boann, and the Seine in France is the goddess Sequana. The ancient Babylonians situated temples to the moon goddess Ishtar in natural grottoes where springs emanated. Many wells and streams are the home of ondines, water nymphs, and other beings.

Sacred springs that bubble up from under the earth have healing properties. The ancient Celts built shrines to the goddess Sulis at the hot mineral waters at Bath, where people have gone to take the waters for seven thousand years. When the Romans later expanded their empire into Britain, they built a temple there to Sulis Minerva. Springs sacred to the goddess Bridget are found throughout Ireland; pilgrims leave offerings and pray to be healed with the water. At the Gallo-Roman *Fontes Sequanae* sanctuary at the source of the Seine, two hundred ancient carved oak figures representing all or part of the human body have been left by people seeking healing. People travel to the Dead Sea to bathe in its waters, which are especially efficacious for healing diseases of the skin.

Water purifies and renews, and it can bring about powerful transformations. Bathing in the sacred River Ganges frees the bather from blemish. It is the custom in most initiatory traditions for the candidate to bathe to ritually purify herself prior to experiencing the mysteries and taking vows. For instance, pilgrims to the Eleusinian Mysteries in ancient Greece purified themselves in the sea prior to initiation.

The river can be a boundary between worlds. The dead must pay a coin to Charon to ferry them across the Underworld River Styx. The bodies of the dead in ancient Egypt were taken from the east to the west side of the Nile for burial on the other side. Throughout the world the dead are washed with clear water to prepare them for the Otherworld. Kanaloa is the old Polynesian sea god of death, darkness, water, and squid.

Some springs, wells, and streams are sources of oracular wisdom. The sacred stream near Demeter's sanctuary at Patras in present-day Jordan provides an infallible divination mirror. Drinking of magical water gives the gift of prophecy.

Today, as we have for thousands of years, we drink water from springs such as Evian and Perrier in France, Pellegrino in Italy, and Calistoga in California for its healthful benefits. Yet in some places the people don't have enough clean drinking water. We have used our oceans as a global garbage dump; we have filled our rivers with contaminants. This desecrates the very source of life. Without a reawakening on the part of all people everywhere to the sacredness of water we as a species will vanish from Earth like six of the Seven Wonders of the Ancient World.

See **Aphrodite, Demeter and Persephone/Kore, Navigation.**

101

White Horse of Uffington

The image of a giant white horse appears on a steep hillside in the English countryside and can be seen for miles across the valley. The site is near an Iron Age hill fort called Uffington Castle in Oxfordshire (formerly Berkshire). This marvelous creation, called the White Horse of Uffington, dates from approximately 50 B.C.E., although newer archaeological techniques date its construction to the late Bronze Age Britain, circa 600–1400 B.C.E., by local Celtic peoples. The turf is carved away from the underlying chalk deposits so that the image emerges in white in stark contrast to the grass growing on the surface, as with the Cerne Abbas Giant in Dorset.

Although the design of the horse is stylized, the image is unmistakably that of a running horse. At 364 feet in length, it is one of the largest figural representative art works on Earth. In local lore, it was called the Dragon's Hill, and it was believed to be the place where St. George killed the dragon (although there's no doubt that the horse was created long before there were saints, dragon-slaying or otherwise).

The horse figures prominently in the mythology, the bardic tradition, and the artwork from early Celtic cultures. Many Celtic tribes had horse goddesses, like Macha of Ireland and Rhiannon of Wales (both usually white horses). The later cult of the horse goddess Epona, also white, originated in Roman Britain, but since the creation of the Uffington Horse predates the Romans, it may be a representation of an earlier horse goddess. Often associated with the sun, horses drew carts or chariots carrying solar images or deities. To the ancient Celts, horses and horse goddesses were also associated with fertility, sovereignty, healing, and death. Similar stylized images of the horse are found on ancient Celtic jewelry and coins.

The Uffington horse was first written about in 1084 C.E. Since at least the year 1650, a festival was held every seven years and lasted up to three days, when people ritually scoured the greenery and the fill of washed-down stone and earth that would encroach into the clean white of the chalk lines. This work was accompanied by wrestling, horse racing and other games, feasting, and merchant's booths. These scourings continued into the twentieth century, with the local people gathering to preserve their Pagan heritage.

See **Cerne Abbas Giant, Emain Macha, Hill of Tara.**

About the Author

M. Macha NightMare, Priestess and Witch, is an author, teacher, and ritualist with a penchant for collaboration. Among the founders of Reclaiming Tradition Witchcraft and an initiate of (Anderson) Faery/Feri Tradition as well, Macha holds Elder and ministerial credentials through the Covenant of the Goddess (CoG), the oldest and largest nondenominational organization of Witches in the United States. A member since 1981, she is a former National First Officer and has served the Covenant in many other capacities. She also is an ordained minister of the Communitarian Church in Vermont. Her writing has appeared in many periodicals, and she has frequently spoken on behalf of NeoPaganism in electronic and print media, at colleges, universities, and seminaries, and in the context of interfaith activities.

She currently serves as chair of the Public Ministry Department of Cherry Hill Seminary in Bethel, Vermont, where she also teaches online courses on dying and death, and on ritual.

Her matron is Kali Ma. Her magical practice is inspired by feminism and a concern for the health of our planet, and is informed by

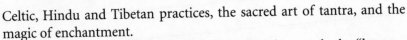

Celtic, Hindu and Tibetan practices, the sacred art of tantra, and the magic of enchantment.

When the opportunity presents itself, Macha travels the "broom-stick circuit," where she enjoys immersing herself in the diverse community that is American Witchcraft. A circuit priestess, Macha is an all-round Pagan webweaver.